# Addressing Special Educational and Disability in the Curriculum: PE and Sports



This topical book provides practical, tried and tested strategies and resources that will support teachers in making PE lessons accessible, rewarding and exciting for all pupils, including those with special needs. The author draws on a wealth of experience to share his understanding of special educational needs and disabilities and show how the PE teacher can reduce or remove any barriers to learning participation.

Offering strategies that are specific to the context of PE and sports teaching, this book will enable teachers to:

- ensure all pupils are able to enjoy and appreciate the value of exercise and sport;
- create an inclusive environment;
- tailor activities to fit the needs of mixed ability groups;
- help pupils to develop the skills and confidence to enjoy different kinds of sport;
- encourage young people to think about what they are doing and make appropriate decisions for themselves.

An invaluable tool for continuing professional development, this text will be essential for teachers, coaches and teaching assistants seeking guidance specific to teaching PE and sport to all pupils, regardless of their individual needs. This book will also be of interest to SENCOs, senior management teams and ITT providers.

With free online material and practical resources in the appendices, this is an essential tool for everyone striving to engage all pupils in PE and sport.

**Crispin Andrews** is a freelance writer and a former PE teacher and sports coach.

**Addressing Special Educational Needs and Disability in the Curriculum**

*Series Editor: Linda Evans*



Children and young people with a diverse range of special educational needs and disabilities (SEND) are expected to access the full curriculum. Crucially, the current professional standards make it clear that *every* teacher must take responsibility for *all* pupils in their classes. Titles in this fully revised and updated series will be essential for teachers seeking subject-specific guidance on meeting their pupils' individual needs. In line with recent curriculum changes, the new Code of Practice for SEN and other pedagogical developments, these titles provide clear, practical strategies and resources that have proved to be effective and successful in their particular subject area. Written by practitioners, they can be used by departmental teams and in 'whole-school' training sessions as professional development resources. With free web-based online resources also available to complement the books, these resources will be an asset to any teaching professional helping to develop policy and provision for learners with SEND.

The new national curriculum content will prove challenging for many learners, and teachers of children in Y5 and Y6 will also find the books a valuable resource.

Titles in this series include:

**Addressing Special Educational Needs and Disability in the Curriculum: Modern Foreign Languages**
*John Connor*

**Addressing Special Educational Needs and Disability in the Curriculum: Music**
*Victoria Jaquiss and Diane Paterson*

**Addressing Special Educational Needs and Disability in the Curriculum: PE and Sports**
*Crispin Andrews*

**Addressing Special Educational Needs and Disability in the Curriculum: Science**
*Marion Frankland*

**Addressing Special Educational Needs and Disability in the Curriculum: Design and Technology**
*Louise T. Davies*

**Addressing Special Educational Needs and Disability in the Curriculum: History**
*Ian Luff and Richard Harris*

**Addressing Special Educational Needs and Disability in the Curriculum: Religious Education**
*Dilwyn Hunt*

**Addressing Special Educational Needs and Disability in the Curriculum: Geography**
*Graeme Eyre*

**Addressing Special Educational Needs and Disability in the Curriculum: Art**
*Kim Earle and Gill Curry*

**Addressing Special Educational Needs and Disability in the Curriculum: English**
*Tim Hurst*

**Addressing Special Educational Needs and Disability in the Curriculum: Maths**
*Max Wallace*

For a full list of titles see: www.routledge.com/series/SENCURR

# Addressing Special Educational Needs and Disability in the Curriculum: PE and Sports

*Second edition*

**Crispin Andrews**

LONDON AND NEW YORK

Second edition published 2018
by Routledge
2 Park Square, Milton Park, Abingdon, Oxon OX14 4RN

and by Routledge
711 Third Avenue, New York, NY 10017

*Routledge is an imprint of the Taylor & Francis Group, an informa business*



First edition published by David Fulton 2005

*British Library Cataloguing in Publication Data*
A catalogue record for this book is available from the British Library

*Library of Congress Cataloging in Publication Data*
A catalog record for this book has been requested

ISBN: 978-1-138-20900-8 (hbk)
ISBN: 978-1-138-20901-5 (pbk)
ISBN: 978-1-315-45797-0 (ebk)

Typeset in Helvetica
by Keystroke, Neville Lodge, Tettenhall, Wolverhampton

Visit the eResources: www.routledge.com/9781138209015

Printed and bound by CPI Group (UK) Ltd, Croydon, CR0 4YY

# Contents

# Appendices

# Series authors

## The author

**Crispin Andrews** is a qualified teacher and sports coach, and has worked extensively in Buckinghamshire schools coaching cricket and football and developing opportunities for girls in these two sports. He is currently a sports journalist, writing extensively for a wide range of educational journals, including *Learning Disability Today* and the *Times Educational Supplement*, and other publications such as *Sports Management* and *Coaching Edge.* For more details, visit his website: www.crispinandrewsfreelancewriter.com.

A dedicated team of SEN specialists and subject specialists have contributed to this series.

## Series editor

**Linda Evans** was commissioning editor for the original books in this series and has coordinated the updating process for these new editions. She has taught children of all ages over the years and posts have included those of SENCO, LA adviser, Ofsted inspector and HE tutor/lecturer. She was awarded a PhD in 2000 following research on improving educational outcomes for children (primary and secondary). Since then, Linda has been commissioning editor for David Fulton Publishing (SEN) as well as editor of a number of educational journals and newsletters; she has also written books, practical classroom resources, Master's course materials and school improvement guidance. She maintains her contact with school practitioners through her work as a part-time ITT tutor and educational consultant.

## SEND specialist

**Sue Briggs** has been supporting the education and inclusion of children with special educational needs and disabilities, and their parents for over twenty years, variously as teacher, Oftsed inspector, specialist member of the SEN and Disability Tribunal, school improvement partner, consultant and adviser. She holds a Master's degree in education, a first class BEd and a diploma in special education (DPSE distinction). Sue was a national lead for the Achievement for All programme (2011–13) and a regional adviser for the Early Support programme for the Council for Disabled Children (2014–15) and is currently an independent education and leadership consultant. Sue is the author of several specialist books and publications including *Meeting SEND in Primary Classrooms* and *Meeting SEND in Secondary Classrooms* (Routledge, 2015).

## Subject specialists

### *Art*

**Gill Curry** was head of art in a secondary school in Wirral for twenty years and advisory teacher for art and gifted and talented strand co-ordinator. She has an MA in print from the University of Chester and an MA in women's studies from the University of Liverpool. She is a practising artist specialising in print and exhibits nationally and internationally, running courses regularly in schools and print studios.

**Kim Earle** is vice principal at Birkenhead High School Academy for Girls on the Wirral. She has previously been a head of art and head of creative arts, securing Artsmark Gold in all the establishments in which she has worked. Kim was also formerly able pupils and arts consultant in St Helens, working across special schools and mainstream schools with teaching and support staff on art policy and practice. She still teaches art in a mixed ability setting in her current school and works closely with local schools and outside organisations to address barriers to learning.

### *Design and technology*

**Louise T. Davies** is founder of the Food Teachers Centre offering advice and guidance to the DfE and other organisations based on her years of experience as a teacher and teacher trainer, and her role in curriculum development at QCA and the Royal College of Art. She led innovation at the Design and Technology Association, providing expertise for a range of curriculum and CPD programmes and specialist advice on teaching standards and best practice, including meeting special educational needs. Most recently, she has worked as lead consultant for the School Food Champions programme (2013–16) and as an adviser to the DfE on the new GCSE in food preparation and nutrition.

## *English*

**Tim Hurst** began his career as an English teacher at the Willian School in Hertfordshire, becoming Second in English before deciding that his future lay in SEND. He studied for an advanced diploma in special educational needs and has been a SEN co-ordinator in five schools in Hertfordshire, Essex and Suffolk. Tim has always been committed to the concept of inclusion and is particularly interested in reading development, which he passionately believes in as a whole-school responsibility.

## *Geography*

**Graeme Eyre** has considerable experience of teaching and leading geography in secondary schools in a range of different contexts, and is currently Assistant Principal for Intervention at an academy in inner London. Graeme is a consultant to the Geographical Association and a Fellow of the Royal Geographical Society. He has also delivered training and CPD for teachers at all levels. He holds a BA in geography, a PGCE in secondary geography and an MA in geography education.

## *History*

**Ian Luff** taught in comprehensive schools for thirty-two years and was head of history in four such schools, writing extensively and delivering training in teaching the subject. He served in the London Borough of Barking and Dagenham as advisory teacher and as deputy headteacher at Kesgrave High School in Suffolk. Ian was made an honorary fellow of the Historical Association for contributions to education in 2011 and is currently an associate tutor and PhD student in the School of Education and Lifelong Learning at the University of East Anglia.

**Richard Harris** taught in comprehensive schools for sixteen years and was a head of history and head of humanities, as well as teacher consultant for history in West Berkshire. He has spent fifteen years working with trainee history teachers at the universities of Southampton and Reading and is currently director of teaching and learning, as well as researching issues mainly relating to history education. He has advised government bodies and worked extensively with the Council of Europe on teacher education and history education. He was made an honorary fellow of the Historical Association in 2011.

## *Maths*

**Max Wallace** has nine years' experience of teaching children with special educational needs. He currently works as an advanced skills teacher at an inclusive mainstream secondary school. Appointed as a specialist leader in education for mathematics, Max mentors and coaches teachers in a wide network of schools. He has previously worked as a head of year and was responsible for the continuing professional development of colleagues. He has a doctorate in mathematics from Cardiff University.

## *Modern foreign languages*

**John Connor** is a former head of faculty, local authority adviser and senior examiner. He has also served as an Ofsted team inspector for modern languages and special educational needs in mainstream settings. John was also an assessor on the Advanced Skills Teacher programme for the DfE. He is currently working as a trainer, author and consultant, and has directed teaching and learning quality audits across England, the Channel Islands, Europe, the Middle East and the Far East. He is also a governor of a local primary school.

## *Music*

**Victoria Jaquiss**, FRSA, trained as a teacher of English and drama and held posts of English teacher, head of PSE, music and expressive arts at Foxwood School. She became a recognised authority on behaviour management and inclusion with children in challenging circumstances. The second half of her career has involved working for the Leeds Music Service/Leeds ArtForms as steel pan development officer and deputy inclusion manager/teacher. She was awarded the fellowship of the Royal Society of Arts in 2002.

**Diane Paterson** began teaching as a mainstream secondary music teacher. She went on to study how music technology could enable people with severe physical difficulties to make their own music, joining the Drake Music project in Yorkshire and becoming its regional leader. She then became inclusion manager/teacher at Leeds Music Service/ArtForms, working with children with additional needs. As secretary of YAMSEN: SpeciallyMusic, she now runs specialist regional workshops, music days and concerts for students with special/additional needs and their carers.

## *Religious education*

**Dilwyn Hunt** taught RE for eighteen years before becoming an adviser first in Birmingham and then in Dudley. He currently works as an independent RE adviser supporting local authorities, SACREs and schools. He is also in demand across the country as a speaker on all aspects of teaching RE, in both mainstream and special settings. He is the author of numerous popular classroom resources and books and currently serves as the executive assistant at the Association of RE Inspectors, Advisers and Consultants.

## *Science*

**Marion Frankland**, CSciTeach, has been teaching for sixteen years and was an advanced skills teacher of science. She has extensive experience of teaching science at all levels, in both mainstream and special schools, and has worked as a SENCO in a special school, gaining her qualification alongside her teaching commitments.

# A few words from the series editor

The original version of this book formed part of the 'Meeting SEN in the Curriculum' series which was published ten years ago to much acclaim. The series won a BERA (British Educational Resources Award) and has been widely used by ITT providers, their students and trainees, curriculum and SEN advisers, department heads and teachers of all levels of experience. It has proven to be highly successful in helping to develop policy and provision for learners with special educational needs or disabilities.

The series was born out of an understanding that practitioners want information and guidance about improving teaching and learning that is *relevant to them* – rooted in their particular subject, and applicable to pupils they encounter. These books exactly fulfil that function.

Those original books have stood the test of time in many ways – their tried and tested, practical strategies are as relevant and effective as ever. Legislation and national guidance have moved on, however, as have resources and technology; new terminology accompanies all of these changes. For example, we have changed the series title to incorporate the acronym 'SEND' (special educational needs and disability) which has been adopted in official documents and in many schools in response to recent legislation and the revised Code of Practice. The important point to make is that our authors have addressed the needs of pupils with a wide range of special or 'additional' needs; some will have Education, Health and Care (EHC) plans which have replaced 'statements', but most will not. Some will have identified 'syndromes' or 'conditions' but many will simply be termed 'low attainers', pupils who, for whatever reason, do not easily make progress.

This second edition encompasses recent developments in education, and specifically in the teaching of PE and sport. At the time of publication, education is still very much in an era of change; our national curriculum, monitoring and assessment systems are all newly fashioned and many schools are still adjusting to changes and developing their own ways forward. The ideas and guidance contained in this book, however, transcend the fluctuations of national politics and policy and provide a framework for ensuring that pupils with SEND can 'enjoy and achieve' in their PE lessons.

NB: The term 'parent' is used throughout and is intended to cover any adult who is a child's main care-giver.

Linda D. Evans

# Acknowledgements

I would like to extend my grateful thanks to the many colleagues who were generous with their time and expertise in providing me with information, ideas and encouragement for the original version of this book and subsequently for this new edition:

Debbie Ashford
Ros Bastian
Mark Botterill
Jason Bridges
Ian Broadbridge
Di Caesar
Sue Campbell
Crichton Casbon
Mike Diaper
Katie Donovan
Lorraine Everard
Steve Grainger
Carol Halpin
Felicity Halsey
Simon Harris
Emma Hughes
Marie Hunter
Angela James
Mike Johnson
Richard Little
Jane McKay
Alison Philpott
Carole Raymond
Anna Robinson
Lynne Spackman
Steve Spiers
Alistair Symondson

Donna Tipping
Jane Tompkins
Dave Tromans
Rob Watson
Richard Whitehead
Tony Willard
Doug Williamson

In addition, my thanks to the following colleagues who contributed to this second edition:

Anne Craddock – SEND PE Consultant
Neil Dawson – Head of PE, Wilson Stuart School
Anna Duberg – Physical Therapist, Orebo University, Sweden
Baroness Tanni Grey-Thompson
Ian Martin – Head of Disability Cricket, England and Wales Cricket Board
Sophia Pittounikos – DS Active Officer and Coach, Down's Syndrome Association

# Introduction

## Ours to teach

**Your class:** thirty individuals to teach – to encourage, motivate and inspire: thirty individuals who must be seen to make good progress regardless of their various abilities, backgrounds, interests and personalities. This is what makes teaching so interesting!

**Jason** demonstrates very little interest in school. He rarely completes homework and frequently turns up without a pen. He finds it hard to listen when you're talking and is likely to start his own conversation with a classmate. His work is untidy and mostly incomplete. It's difficult to find evidence of his progress this year.

**Zoe** tries very hard in lessons but is slow to understand explanations and has difficulty in expressing herself. She has been assessed as having poor communication skills but there is no additional resourcing for her.

**Ethan** is on the autistic spectrum and finds it difficult to relate to other people, to work in a group and to understand social norms. He has an education, health and care plan which provides for some TA support but this is not timetabled for all lessons.

Do you recognise these youngsters? Our school population is now more diverse than ever before, with pupils of very different abilities, aptitudes and interests, from a wide range of cultures, making up our mainstream and special school classes. Many of these learners will experience difficulties of some sort at school, especially when they are faced with higher academic expectations at the end of KS2 and into KS3–4.

Whether they have a specific special educational need like dyslexia, or are on the autistic spectrum, or for various reasons cannot conform to our behavioural expectations – *they are ours to teach*. Our lessons must ensure that each and every pupil can develop their skills and knowledge and make good progress.

## How can this book help?

The information, ideas and guidance in this book will enable coaches and teachers of PE and sport (and their teaching assistants) to plan and deliver lessons that will meet the individual needs of learners who experience difficulties. It will be especially valuable because the ideas and guidance are provided within the subject context, ensuring relevance and practicability.

Teachers who cater well for pupils with special educational needs and disabilities (SEND) are likely to cater well for *all* pupils – demonstrating outstanding practice in their everyday teaching. These teachers have a keen awareness of the many factors affecting a pupil's ability to learn, not only characteristics of the individual but also aspects of the learning environment that can either help or hinder learning. This book will help practitioners to develop strategies that can be used selectively to enable each and every learner to make progress.

## Professional development

Our education system is constantly changing. The national curriculum, SEND legislation, examination reform and significant change to Ofsted inspection mean that teachers need to keep up to date and be able to develop the knowledge, skills and understanding necessary to meet the needs of all the learners they teach. High-quality continuing professional development (CPD) has a big part to play in this.

Faculties and subject teams planning for outstanding teaching and learning should consider how they regularly review and improve their provision by:

- auditing:

    a) the skills and expertise of current staff (teachers and assistants);
    b) their professional development needs for SEND, based on the current cohorts of pupils;

    (An audit proforma can be found in the eResources at: www.routledge.com/9781138209015)

- using the information from the two audits to develop a CPD programme (using internal staff, colleagues from nearby schools and/or consultants to deliver bespoke training);

- enabling teachers to observe each other, teach together, visit other classrooms and other schools;
- encouraging staff to reflect on their practice and feel comfortable in sharing both the positive and the negative experiences;
- establishing an ethos that values everyone's expertise (including pupils and parents who might be able to contribute to training sessions);
- using online resources that are readily available to support workforce development (e.g. www.nasen.org.uk/onlinesendcpd/);
- encouraging staff to access (and disseminate) further study and high quality professional development.

This book, and the others in the series, will be invaluable in contributing to whole-school CPD on meeting special educational needs, and in facilitating subject-specific staff development within departments.

# 1 Meeting special educational needs and disabilities

## Your responsibility

New legislation and national guidance in 2014 changed the landscape of educational provision for pupils with any sort of 'additional' or 'special' needs. The vast majority of learners, including those with 'moderate' or 'mild' learning difficulties, weak communication skills, dyslexia or social/behavioural needs, rarely attract additional resources; they are very much accepted as part of the 'mainstream mix'. Pupils with more significant special educational needs and/or disabilities (SEND) may have an Education, Health and Care plan (EHC plan): this outlines how particular needs will be met, often involving professionals from different disciplines, and sometimes specifying adult support in the classroom. Both groups of pupils are ultimately the responsibility of the class teacher, whether in mainstream or special education.

> High quality teaching that is differentiated and personalised will meet the individual needs of the majority of children and young people. Some children and young people need educational provision that is additional to or different from this. This is special educational provision under Section 21 of the Children and Families Act 2014. Schools and colleges *must* use their best endeavours to ensure that such provision is made for those who need it. Special educational provision is underpinned by high quality teaching and is compromised by anything less.
>
> SEND Code of Practice (DfE 2015)

There is more information about legislation (the Children and Families Act 2014; the Equality Act 2010) and guidance (SEND Code of Practice) in Appendix 1.

## Definition of SEND

A pupil has special educational needs if he or she:

- has a significantly greater difficulty in learning than the majority of others of the same age; or
- has a disability which prevents or hinders him or her from making use of facilities of a kind generally provided for others of the same age in mainstream schools or mainstream post-16 institutions.

(SEND Code of Practice 2015)

The SEND Code of Practice identifies four broad areas of SEND, but remember that this gives only an overview of the range of needs that should be planned for by schools; pupils' needs rarely fit neatly into one area of need only.

## Whole-school ethos

Successful schools are proactive in identifying and addressing pupils' special needs, focusing on adapting the educational context and environment rather than on 'fixing' an individual learner. Adapting systems and teaching programmes rather than trying to force the pupil to conform to rigid expectations will lead to a greater chance of success in terms of learning outcomes. Guidance on whole-school and departmental policy making can be found in

*Table 1.1* The four broad areas of SEND

| *Communication and interaction* | *Cognition and learning* | *Social, emotional and mental health difficulties* | *Sensory and/or physical needs* |
|---|---|---|---|
| Speech, language and communication needs (SLCN) | Specific learning difficulties (SpLD) | Mental health difficulties such as anxiety or depression, self-harming, substance abuse or eating disorders | Vision impairment (VI) |
| Asperger's Syndrome and Autism (ASD) | Moderate learning difficulties (MLD) | | Hearing impairment (HI) |
| | | | Multi-sensory impairment (MSI) |
| | Severe learning difficulties (SLD) | Attention deficit disorders, attention deficit hyperactivity disorder or attachment disorder | Physical disability (PD) |
| | Profound and multiple learning difficulties (PMLD) | | |

Appendix 2 and a sample departmental policy for SEND can be downloaded from the eResources at www.routledge.com/9781138209015.

## Policy into practice

In many cases, pupils' individual learning needs will be met through differentiation of tasks and materials in their lessons; sometimes this will be supplemented by targeted interventions such as literacy 'catch-up' programmes delivered outside the classroom, or sessions designed to improve motor skills and co-ordination. A smaller number of pupils may need access to more specialist equipment and approaches, perhaps based on advice and support from external specialists.

The main thrust of the Children and Families Act and Chapter 6 of the SEND Code of Practice is that outcomes for pupils with SEND must be improved and that schools and individual teachers must have high aspirations and expectations for all.

In practice, this means that pupils should be enabled to:

- **achieve their best**; additional provision made for pupils with SEND will enable them to make accelerated progress so that the gap in progress and attainment between them and other pupils is reduced. Being identified with SEND should no longer be a reason for a pupil making less than good progress.
- **become confident individuals living fulfilling lives**; if you ask parents of children with SEND what is important to them for their child's future, they often answer 'happiness, the opportunity to achieve his or her potential, friendships and a loving family' – just what we all want for our children. Outcomes in terms of wellbeing, social skills and growing independence are equally as important as academic outcomes for children and young people with SEND.
- **make a successful transition into adulthood, whether into employment, further or higher education or training;** decisions made at transition from primary school, in Year 7 and beyond should be made in the context of preparation for adulthood. For example, where a pupil has had full-time support from a teaching assistant in primary school, the secondary school's first reaction might be to continue this level of support after transition. This may result in long-term dependency on adults, however, or limited opportunities to develop social skills, both of which impact negatively on preparation for adulthood.

## Excellent day-to-day provision

Later chapters provide lots of subject-specific ideas and guidance on strategies to support pupils with SEND. In Appendix 3 you will find useful checklists to help you support pupils with identified 'conditions', but there are some generic approaches that form the foundations of outstanding provision, such as:

- providing support from adults or other pupils;
- adapting tasks or environments;
- using specialist aids and equipment as appropriate.

The starting points listed below provide a sound basis for creating an inclusive learning environment that will benefit *all* pupils, while being especially important for those with SEND.

**Develop pupils' understanding through the use of all available senses by:**

- using resources that pupils can access through sight *and* sound (and where appropriate also use the senses of touch, taste and smell to broaden understanding and ensure stronger memory);
- regularly employing resources such as symbols, pictures and film to increase pupils' knowledge and contextualise new information and skills;
- encouraging and enabling pupils to take part in as wide a range of activities as possible.

**Help pupils to learn effectively and prepare for further or higher education, work or training by:**

- setting realistic demands within high expectations;
- using positive strategies to manage behaviour;
- giving pupils opportunities and encouragement to develop the skills to work effectively in a group or with a partner;
- teaching all pupils to value and respect the contribution of others;
- encouraging independent working skills;
- teaching essential safety rules.

**Help pupils to develop communication skills, language and literacy by:**

- making sure all pupils can see your face when you are speaking;
- giving clear, step-by-step instructions, and limiting the amount of information given at one time;
- explaining key vocabulary for each lesson;
- making text available in different formats, including large text or symbols, or by using screen-reader programs;

- presenting written information as concisely as possible, using bullet points, images or diagrams.

**Support pupils with disabilities by:**

- encouraging pupils to be as independent as possible;
- enabling them to work with other, non-disabled pupils;
- making sure the environment is suitable, e.g. uncluttered space to facilitate movement; adapted equipment that is labelled and accessible;
- being aware that some pupils will take longer to complete tasks;
- taking into account the higher levels of concentration and physical exertion required by some pupils that will lead to increased fatigue for pupils who may already have reduced stamina;
- ensuring all pupils are included, and can participate safely, in a wide variety of sport and exercise activities, school trips and off-site visits.

These and other more specific strategies are placed in the context of supporting particular individuals described in the case studies featured throughout the book.

# 2 Creating an inclusive environment for PE and sport

> I still hear of young people missing PE lessons because they're told that they can't do it. I find it harder to locate children for the Birmingham disability athletics team that I run than ever before.
>
> Neil Dawson, head of PE, Wilson Stuart School

There's more to creating an inclusive learning environment for PE and sport than buying a few sets of boccia balls and making sure the sports hall has wheelchair access.

The *Oxford English Dictionary* defines 'environment' as the surroundings or conditions in which a person lives or operates, or the setting or conditions in which a particular activity is carried on. According to Wikipedia, the term 'learning environment' is about cultural context and prevailing educational approaches, as well as the physical setting in which teaching and learning takes place. It's also about the interactions which take place within that environment.

Unfortunately, young people with special educational needs and disabilities often find it difficult to operate successfully within their learning environment. This is not their fault. It's more that to be successful within that environment often requires them to do things they can't do, which in turn takes focus away from the things they *can* do. To make the learning environment inclusive, this dynamic between young person and learning environment needs to be turned on its head.

That's easier said than done. There's so much within the learning environment that a PE teacher can't control, even a really good teacher with lots of experience, training and a real commitment to getting everyone learning, active and reaching their potential. You may be committed to inclusion, but not all departmental colleagues will necessarily agree. And even if they do, the school leadership might set its priorities away from inclusive PE and sport, especially with the recent focus on academic progress.

A PE teacher can't make feeder primaries or local sports clubs and community groups provide inclusive opportunities. Nor can they ensure parents, carers and other support workers are supportive of a young person's physical activity and sporting choices, or even make sure young people, in their time away from school and homework, put their iPhones, laptops and games consoles down for long enough to even think about doing a bit of sport.

The chances of getting any sort of reasoned debate about the pros and cons of inclusive sport and physical education into the popular consciousness are pretty remote. When the Paralympics is on, there is more interest of course, or if someone in the public eye says something stupid or offensive about disabled people playing sport. Forgive me for listing the negatives! Let's now look more positively at the situation.

We can make a diagram where a young person's learning environment for PE and sport is represented as a series of concentric circles, with the young person at the centre. Within each circle there are challenges, barriers to that young person getting some high-quality physical education and sport and really benefiting from it. But there are also opportunities, where teachers, coaches and instructors can help the young person.

Within the second circle sit school PE, staff, infrastructure and the other young people in the class. Then there's the school itself, its ethos and culture. Next, the young person's immediate support network, their family, friends and carers. Then the local area, how it's made up, what opportunities there are. Then you get on to wider society and government. Each 'layer' will influence the young person's experience, either directly or indirectly.

## Inclusion

Inclusion isn't just about making sure young people with special educational needs and disabilities get a decent chance; it's actually about helping each and every person, whatever their ability, to have a beneficial experience.

Good teachers already do this. Every day they set learning tasks that challenge and stretch individual children. Things work less well when teachers teach to lowest common denominators, be that perceived group abilities, or to the rules of a particular sport or activity and the necessary skill sets to play it. That's when young people with needs that are a bit different can be excluded (and that includes more able young people, or youngsters who already know the rules of a particular game).

Trying to create an inclusive environment in a place where it doesn't already exist will bring teachers into conflict with the protectors of the status quo. This group includes those teachers who aren't really interested in PE; the head of PE whose reputation has been built on the success of his rugby and football teams; the head teacher to whom exam results are all that matters; the local authority bigwig whose popularity is secured only by the promotion of a school-centred vision of education; the non-doing sports development officer schooled in the days of pen pushing and self-perpetuation; and the hockey club chairman who is only interested in talent spotting and inviting the best youngsters to his club.

The list goes on. And under pressure from these people, all of whom will be chanting, 'If it ain't broke don't fix it', the job of the creative innovator, eager to provide a more inclusive learning environment for their students, becomes more difficult.

> There's always pressure on children with SEND to do some extra maths or English work during their games lessons rather than take part in an activity that might be really good for them. And these are young people who could take part in a Paralympic sport, maybe to a high level.
>
> Neil Dawson, head of PE, Wilson Stuart School

> Other kids have to understand that the young person with SEN might take longer to complete a task than they do. Make that an enhancement to the game that everyone is playing, rather than an interference. So, in an invasion game, the team has to get the ball to the young person with Down's Syndrome last, before they can score a point. Then, the other young people have to support the young person with the SEN.
>
> Sophia Pittounikos, DS Active Officer and coach,
> Down's Syndrome Association

## *The physical environment*

In spite of recent improvements and extensions to schools, many were designed and built at a time when there was little consideration given to the idea or practicalities of 'inclusion'. The fabric and design of buildings and outside areas routinely present a number of issues for staff to consider:

- Is it physically possible for wheelchair users to be included when their class is timetabled to use a muddy field in the middle of winter?
- Are there two doormats strategically positioned outside the entrance to the changing rooms to stop wheelchairs bringing mud into the school and facing the combined wrath of caretaker and head teacher?

- The school's new Astroturf has just been given a £3,000 facelift. Will the head of department allow wheelchairs to buzz around all over it?
- Could sports halls where sun streams in through the windows create blind spots for a child with cerebral palsy, increasing the risk of dangerous collisions?
- Are new sports halls built with smaller adjacent halls so that parallel indoor activities with smaller groups don't have to take place in a corridor or cloakroom?
- Is the presence of thirteen different sets of markings on the floor of the hall likely to assist or confuse the understanding of children with cognitive difficulties or colour blindness?
- Do boards for basketball and netball have to be set, or would adjustable boards fit a wider range of needs?
- Are all pegs in the changing rooms at eye height or are some dropped lower to make it easier for wheelchair users to reach them?
- Are there discreet changing areas for those children who need assistance, so that they do not feel the spotlight is on them?
- Are there toilets big enough for wheelchair users and is there an assistance rail for those who need it?
- Is insisting on white shorts as part of a school uniform any more likely to encourage children with continence needs to want to take part than making these individuals stand out by allowing them to wear black instead?
- Is there signage to clearly show children how to get from the changing rooms to the gym and the outdoor playing area?

## *Inclusive learning environment – how can we tell?*

There are many different ways a school can develop an inclusive learning environment for PE and sport. It can:

- make PE and sport a central part of young people's lives in and out of school;
- know and understand what young people are trying to achieve and how to go about doing it;
- understand that PE and sport are an important part of an active, healthy lifestyle;
- help young people develop the confidence to get involved;
- help them to develop the skills and control to take part successfully;
- encourage young people to:
    - take part willingly in a range of group and individual activities;
    - think about what they are doing and make appropriate decisions for themselves;
    - show a desire to improve and achieve in relation to their own abilities;

- develop the stamina, suppleness and strength to keep going;
- enjoy PE, school and community sport.

Above all, if a learning environment is truly inclusive, it will enable young people to feel comfortable, motivated, empowered and appreciated, and able to give of their best. This means listening to them and paying attention to what they say.

Do that and you'll find out what young people themselves think about their own physical activity needs, what their expectations are and what they think about their school. You might discover that some young people want to feel a greater sense of belonging, or have leadership opportunities, maybe more fun and excitement.

The aspirations, self-esteem and motivation of pupils with conditions such as ADHD and ASD could be raised by incorporating more opportunities for creativity, curiosity, fun and leadership into lessons. This could be achieved by delivering lessons with more open-ended tasks which allow pupils to decide on how they want to demonstrate learning outcomes. For example, while one group involved in a creative movement lesson might wish to show their end product to the rest of the class, another might prefer to put their sequence to music, but to operate at the same time as other groups were working and be observed only by the teacher. A third group might simply wish to report back orally, demonstrating an understanding of the learning that had taken place in their own way.

The next step could be for young people to become more involved in deciding how their particular style of learning could be incorporated into task design. While some are motivated by competing against their peers, for others the extra pressure inhibits both performance and progress. Some work better on their own than in a large group.

If the lesson focus is generic rather than sport or skill specific, it is possible to incorporate a variety of activities to cater for different learning styles, and better still for young people to develop their own activities. This would give them another chance to be creative, facilitate independent learning and instil a greater sense of ownership over the outcomes.

The teacher's role here would be to monitor the nature of the activity to ensure that it enabled every child to focus on the core objectives of the lesson and that activities didn't simply turn into a free-for-all, with fun and enjoyment the only outcome.

Older pupils with conditions such as ADHD could work with, and support, younger pupils with the same condition. This might enable both age groups to take ownership of their behaviour, build their self-confidence and self-esteem and improve their performance. Such a mentoring system would help both mentors and mentees to identify their own strengths and set goals relating to their individual learning targets. The older mentors might also help the other students by demonstrating how best they can work with learning support assistants to develop their own learning strategies and to track their acquisition of key skills.

## What makes an inclusive PE teacher?

There can be differences in how people perceive the word 'inclusive'. It can mean something different for a professional care worker, a family member, sports group and an individual with learning difficulties. If you're new to a PE department, or you're bringing in an external deliverer, a coach or an instructor, or if you're sending a young person off site to a sports session, it is important to know, beforehand, what the word 'inclusion' means to everyone involved. Then you can gauge expectations and try to ensure that the teacher, coaches, instructors and young people involved are in agreement about what will happen in the sessions.

> Everyone has the intention of being inclusive, but are we finding ways of making sure that provision is for all – a life changing experience for every child, no matter what their ability and aspiration? We must do more than simply increase opportunities for those children who already love sport, we must find ways of engaging new children. Not just because we want more to do PE and sport, but because we want the best life chances for all of them and believe that PE and sport can contribute to this.
>
> Sue Campbell, Chair of the Youth Sport Trust

An inclusive PE teacher would be someone who:

- listens to pupils in order to gauge needs, expectations and wants;
- values the progress and achievement of all, while helping children understand what progress is;
- challenges their own existing practice in order that their delivery might engage a wider range of pupils.

### Case study – Elliot, a pupil with achondraplasia (abnormally short stature)

Elliot, a youngster with a condition known as achondraplasia (a form of dwarfism), loved sport, even though there was much his condition prevented him from doing. Elliot was a fantastic footballer with highly developed skills, but he couldn't keep up with his peers when involved in a game. Their physical advantages enabled them to run faster, turn more quickly and jump higher. Contact sports like rugby were impossible for Elliot, due to his spinal weaknesses. He was easily knocked over and it was important to keep his back injury-free.

Like many boys of his age, Elliot was lazy. Finding exercise a chore, he was beginning to put on weight, which caused his back even more problems. As he got older, he began to rely more and more on his learning support assistant to help him muddle through PE lessons.

The summer term meant athletics. Long distance running! The fifteen hundred metres! Collective moans! Sudden epidemics of stomach bugs, hay fever and doctor's notes! Although initially reluctant, Elliot decided that he would do the 1500 m.

He struggled. But, accompanied by his LSA (learning support assistant) – who carried round a bottle of water to make sure not too much fluid was lost (his condition made him prone to sweating) on his way round – Elliot made it. While others had weaselled out of taking part, Elliot had completed the 1500 m. News travels quickly around a school. Other PE staff and teachers from other departments soon found out about his achievements. For the first time, Elliot was being singled out for praise, congratulated on his effort. For a child who compared his own perceived shortcomings to the greater proficiencies of his peers, the sense of accomplishment he felt was immense.

From then on, Elliot's attitude to PE changed. Even when he found something difficult, he was confident enough to give it a go. His peers, many of whom had previously 'not wanted to go with the dwarf' in partner or group situations, began to accept him as part of the class. From this, he developed a greater sense of belonging, which impacted upon his whole school life. Gradually he became a more confident pupil willing to give of his best in all sorts of other situations.

Carol Halpin, former inclusive PE and sport development officer with the Nottinghamshire Sports Disability Unit, describes how listening to an individual helped that student overcome her inhibitions and engage with PE:

> Whilst visiting a school, I saw one particular girl sitting at the side during what was one of her first PE lessons, as the rest of her Year 7 class were playing netball. I asked Naomi why she was not taking part and she said she wasn't feeling well. Further questioning eventually revealed that, at her primary school, Naomi had been hit in the face by a ball while practising throwing and catching. It transpired not only that she did not want to do PE any more, but that she had got herself so worked up that she had refused to come to school unless her parents wrote her a note excusing her from PE lessons.
>
> A few weeks later when I saw the same girl happily taking part in the lesson, I asked the teacher what had happened to change her tune. Previously, Naomi, who has co-ordination difficulties, simply couldn't cope with the sort of fast-paced game of netball during which she had been struck. She felt that she had neither the technique nor the agility to prevent herself being hit again. However, when the class was broken down into smaller ability groups and Naomi was the one chosen from her group to select from a range of balls, not only could she choose a softer ball, one which she felt safe with, but she also felt empowered that it was 'her' game.
>
> For the first time, she was taking ownership of her own learning environment. Here she could begin to develop basic skills without fear of injury and progress at her own speed to a point where she is now confident and proficient enough to play games like netball and basketball with a harder ball. All this had happened simply because the teacher had been willing to listen to the child, find out what was preventing her from joining in and apply a solution to that problem which did not make the child feel she was being singled out.

## Valuing the progress of all

> Winning should be about being better today, than you were yesterday.
>
> Frank Dick

Young people have a natural tendency to compare themselves to the best performer in the group and find a relative place for themselves in the hierarchy. How many times do you hear things like 'Watch out for him – he's really good' or 'Don't worry about her – she's useless' only to find that the teacher's perception of what is good and not so good doesn't match that of the pupils?

Often it is the person who looks good, can do something flash, run the fastest or hit a ball the hardest or the furthest who is considered the best by their peers. The more thoughtful, controlled performer and the awkward-looking youngster come right down at the bottom on the street-cred scale. It is up to teachers and coaches to challenge this comparative, outcome-based notion of success and to ensure that everyone's progress is registered and the efforts of all are valued.

For children to value progress, they need to understand what it is and see for themselves when it has happened. Everyone comes into a specific situation with a certain level of experience, technical development, natural ability and potential to develop at a certain speed. Progress for one pupil will not necessarily look the same as progress for another.

Who has done the best in a lesson? There might be a club standard swimmer who cruises through a series of lessons and easily beats everyone in the race, but who is unable to hit her own self-improvement targets. Through lack of effort, she doesn't improve the co-ordination of her leg and arm movements, or significantly eradicate the sideways rolling motion which is affecting her forward momentum, causing her to expend greater levels of energy for less speed. Then there is the young person who at the start of the module is unable to swim at all but after five weeks can swim ten metres unaided – albeit with a pretty basic technique. We need to look at starting points before we can accurately measure real progress.

Photo: Simon Harris

If progress is relative to one's own performance, everyone can be a 'winner'. But youngsters may not see this and will need it explained and reinforced through regular discussion during lessons. Progress can be about improving performance, but it can also be about developing a technique or increasing concentration or awareness. For some pupils it might be about having the confidence to take part or simply enjoying themselves for the first time.

Convincing pupils that learning is about self-improvement is a major challenge. Some pupils never get past the idea that they are only trying at school to impress family and friends. Some want nothing to do with self-improvement, seeing it as co-operating with a system they hold in low regard. Still other pupils avoid any thought of bettering themselves because they are so afraid of failure. In physical activities, unlike most written tasks, failure is often on public display, so promoting the idea of self-improvement is a key area of engagement for the PE teacher committed to inclusion.

Often youngsters don't progress as quickly as they could during a lesson, but when this happens, it is still possible to turn a negative into a positive. The teacher might, for example, say:

> Yes, you under-performed in that particular game and you may feel disappointed and think you have let your team or yourself down. But if you can work out what it is that has caused you to perform below your best and decide what you will try and do next time to put that right, then you have learnt from your mistakes. You now have a greater awareness of and hence more control over your performance. In other words you have progressed during the lesson. You have done well!

## Challenge, innovation and change

Anyone, whatever their profession or vocation, will stagnate if they simply stand still. After Roger Bannister had achieved the impossible and broken the four-minute mile, a whole host of other athletes soon bettered his time. Now four-minute miles are the norm for top athletes, who are constantly updating their training methods just to gain that extra edge over their rivals.

When developing teaching and learning strategies, organising timetables and deciding on priorities, ask yourself:

- Have we identified and are we employing the key enabling factors that allow our school to adopt innovation and take advantage of opportunities for more youngsters to play sport?
- Are systems in place within our school that allow our staff the necessary time to carry out their roles properly?

- Are mechanisms in place to allow us to share good practice from within and outside the school?
- Is the local educational ethos up to date? Are key personnel aware of, or sympathetic towards, PE and school sport? If not, then how can department and school leaders proactively disseminate the sort of messages necessary to alter attitudes?

(See Appendix 4 and the eResources at www.routledge.com/9781138209015 for a strategic planner for effective inclusion.)

# 3 Teaching and learning

For most adults, sport is like Marmite. You either love it or hate it, or are completely indifferent to it. Often people's attitudes towards sport are formed not necessarily by their first experiences of PE at school, but by their last or most recent.

## From daisy chains to drill camp

Consider for a moment the idyllic setting of the traditional primary school. It is a lovely summer's afternoon and, for a special treat, Mrs North-North-East has decided that the class is to play a game of rounders. After an extended silent reading session, where teacher marks maths books and Felicity and Fleur take round the book-club leaflets to the other classes, the children change for PE, in their own good time of course, and take a leisurely stroll over to the field.

The nice lady in the office asks Felicity and Fleur if they would mind watering the plants around the school after they have finished handing out their leaflets. 'Of course you can, girls,' beams Mrs Fussleworth-Potts. 'You're only missing PE.' Out on the field, the children spend the next twenty minutes arguing about who's going in what team, but, eventually, the actual PE begins. If you can call it that.

Nobody notices when Torquil and Tarquin, the twins, spend the first five minutes making daisy chains and dreaming about their pet bunny rabbit, Fluffy. After someone hits the ball worryingly close to their tranquil little safe haven, they sidle quietly up to their teacher. 'We're cold,' moans Torquil. 'And my tummy hurts,' Tarquin adds. Mrs Fussleworth-Potts looks up into the skies. One cloud. 'Well I must admit it is getting a bit parky out here,' she says. The teacher had forgotten to bring out her favourite Marks and Spencer's cardigan. 'OK children!' she announces. 'Let's go inside, before it starts to rain.'

Sohail, Susan and Stuart, who had all been looking forward to doing PE for the first time in about three weeks, look at each other wryly. 'My dad was right,'

Stuart says. 'PE and school sport is rubbish. At least I'm going to football down the road later tonight.' Sohail and Susan look sad. Both would love to go to football too, but girls are not allowed to join the club so Susan cannot go, and Sohail's dad is working and so can't get him there.

Fleur, Felicity, Torquil and Tarquin skip happily back to the classroom for a bit of extra silent reading. Imagine the looks on their faces, a year down the line, though. They've moved on to secondary school and are lined up in the pouring rain for their first cross-country lesson, wearing nothing but uniform cotton T-shirts and shorts. The coddling Mrs Fussleworth-Potts is a distant memory, replaced by PE teachers Herr Von Sternauss and Ms Spiky, who are barking out orders like prison warders. 'There'll be no sore tummies, daisy chains and book-club leaflets today, me laddoes!'

Exaggerated stereotypes perhaps. We know that PE is a requirement of the national curriculum (2014) for all Key Stages, but we also know that in practice it is not always seen as being important in the way that English and maths are important. Two serious questions can be posed from all of this:

1. What are we trying to achieve from our teaching of PE and sport?
2. Is the sudden transition from the 'optional fun' of primary PE to 'compulsory learning' at secondary school responsible for the disengagement of many youngsters?

**Key Stage 1**

Pupils should develop fundamental movement skills, become increasingly competent and confident and access a broad range of opportunities to extend their agility, balance and coordination, individually and with others. They should be able to engage in competitive (both against self and against others) and co-operative physical activities, in a range of increasingly challenging situations.

Pupils should be taught to:

- master basic movements including running, jumping, throwing and catching, as well as developing balance, agility and co-ordination, and begin to apply these in a range of activities
- participate in team games, developing simple tactics for attacking and defending
- perform dances using simple movement patterns

**Key Stage 2**

Pupils should continue to apply and develop a broader range of skills, learning how to use them in different ways and to link them to make actions and sequences of movement. They should enjoy communicating, collaborating and competing with each other. They should develop an understanding of how to improve in different physical activities and sports and learn how to evaluate and recognise their own success.

Pupils should be taught to:

- use running, jumping, throwing and catching in isolation and in combination
- play competitive games, modified where appropriate [for example, badminton, basketball, cricket, football, hockey, netball, rounders and tennis], and apply basic principles suitable for attacking and defending

- develop flexibility, strength, technique, control and balance [for example, through athletics and gymnastics]
- perform dances using a range of movement patterns
- take part in outdoor and adventurous activity challenges both individually and within a team
- compare their performances with previous ones and demonstrate improvement to achieve their personal best

**Swimming and water safety**

All schools must provide swimming instruction either in KS 1 or KS 2. In particular, pupils should be taught to:

- swim competently, confidently and proficiently over a distance of at least 25 metres
- use a range of strokes effectively [for example, front crawl, backstroke and breaststroke]
- perform safe self-rescue in different water-based situations

**Key Stage 3**

Pupils should build on and embed the physical development and skills learned in Key Stages 1 and 2, become more competent, confident and expert in their techniques, and apply them across different sports and physical activities. They should understand what makes a performance effective and how to apply these principles to their own and others' work. They should develop the confidence and interest to get involved in exercise, sports and activities out of school and in later life, and understand and apply the long-term health benefits of physical activity. Pupils should be taught to:

- use a range of tactics and strategies to overcome opponents in direct competition through team and individual games [for example, badminton, basketball, cricket, football, hockey, netball, rounders, rugby and tennis]
- develop their technique and improve their performance in other competitive sports [e.g. athletics and gymnastics]
- perform dances using advanced dance techniques in a range of dance styles and forms
- take part in outdoor and adventurous activities which present intellectual and physical challenges and be encouraged to work in a team, building on trust and developing skills to solve problems, individually or as a group
- analyse their performances compared to previous ones and demonstrate improvement to achieve their personal best
- take part in competitive sports and activities outside school through community links or sports clubs

**Key Stage 4**

Pupils should tackle complex and demanding physical activities. They should get involved in a range of activities that develops personal fitness and promotes an active, healthy lifestyle. Pupils should be taught to:

- use and develop a variety of tactics and strategies to overcome opponents in team and individual games [as above]
- develop their technique and improve their performance in other competitive sports [e.g. athletics & gymnastics] or other physical activities [for example, dance]
- take part in further outdoor and adventurous activities in a range of environments which present intellectual and physical challenges and which encourage pupils to work in a team, building on trust and developing skills to solve problems, either individually or as a group
- evaluate their performances compared to previous ones and demonstrate improvement across a range of physical activities to achieve their personal best
- continue to take part regularly in competitive sports and activities outside school (as above) .

NB: Schools are not required by law to teach the example content in [square brackets].

*Figure 3.1* National curriculum in England: physical education programmes of study (DFE-00176-2013, KS 1 and 2, and DFE-00176-2013, KS 3 and 4), www.gov.uk/government/uploads/system/uploads/attachment_data/file/239086/SECONDARY_national_curriculum_-_Physical_education.pdf

## Inclusion or performance?

Does it have to be one or the other? If we focus teaching and learning on individual needs and not lowest common denominators, then everybody, whatever their abilities, can perform, develop and benefit from PE and sport.

> People sometimes don't realise that young people in wheelchairs can throw a javelin, shot putt and discus; and they can sprint.
>
> Neil Dawson, head of PE, Wilson Stuart School

Sport is competitive, but PE doesn't have to be. We can get individuals to focus on self-improvement if we behave like a coach in training rather than a coach in a game situation. The problem is that the sport we see and talk about is competitive by its very nature. In professional sport, if players don't perform as well as other players, in their own teams and in opposition teams, they get dropped. So too if they perform worse than is expected, or make a mistake that leads to their team losing. Then everyone starts analysing the player and, before you know it, a player who used to be flavour of the month is suddenly ready for the scrap heap. Then, if they play a couple of good games, or the team starts winning again, everyone forgets their little blip.

This culture can rub off on PE and school sport. Winning matches, scoring points, runs or goals, learning rules, running a certain time or playing a certain position well – all of these are important in competitive sport, but when they become the defining principles in school, individuals' learning needs can be hijacked by the need for 'a win'. The Sohails, Susans and Stuarts of this world will always find their way in PE and school sport. But the curriculum is broad enough that even the terrible twins and the perennial plant waterers can and should also benefit.

> The current PE curriculum dumbed down to the point where you can do anything, or not do anything. I still meet young people who do no PE at all.
>
> Anne Craddock, SEND PE consultant

We want young people to remain focused on their own development, understanding that small steps of improvement can be as significant as large ones are for others. These steps might be about getting better at a sport or a particular skill, but equally might be about becoming more confident or realising that it's possible to take part in, and enjoy, an activity they've never done before – meeting new people, making friends and joining in with non-disabled peers.

(See Chapter 4 for details of the P scales which outline performance descriptors suitable for some pupils with SEND.)

## Considerations when planning inclusive PE sessions

### *Know your students and their individual needs*

Gather information from colleagues, the SENCO, pupil records and students themselves at the earliest opportunity to inform your planning and enable you to differentiate appropriately.

### *Have high expectations*

Communicate these to pupils by sharing with them the lesson objectives. Make sure your objectives are:

- clearly defined, using pupil-friendly action words (see list below);
- measurable, in terms of time, distance, level of skill, frequency/reliability etc., in ways that show progress against previous personal best;
- differentiated to meet a range of needs (use the must, should, could model or use different active verbs to make objectives more challenging, e.g. demonstrate/describe/compare/evaluate . . . running with a rugby ball).

These active verbs can be used to state clear learning objectives:

| **To show knowledge and understanding: to be able to . . .** | **To show skill development: to be able to…** |
|---|---|
| analyse, argue, arrange, assess, calculate, characterise, circle, cite, classify, compare, consider, contrast, criticise, | adapt, adjust, adopt, assemble, choose, collect, demonstrate, employ, establish |
| define, demonstrate, describe, draw, evaluate, give examples | illustrate, imitate, interact, locate, maintain, manage, model, manipulate |
| group, identify, interpret, label, list, justify | master, measure, modify, operate, organise, perform, practise |
| match, name, number, outline, plan, prepare, position | rearrange, select, set up, use |
| recommend, record, recognise, revise, select, solve, state, suggest, tabulate | |

### *Limit teacher-talk*

Resist the temptation to talk too much: pupils switch off after about ten minutes and become fidgety. Plan your explanation carefully, deliver it succinctly and then move into the pupil activity stage of the session. Pupils who need more explanation can opt to 'hear it all again' – perhaps from a TA or a voice recording; use visual back-up to support them if possible.

### *Check understanding/progression*

Show what 'good' looks like through exemplars and/or clear modelling. In PE this could be a specific skill, a passage of play or a compositional idea. Defined teaching points are key to checking for understanding and progress. These should be used for each skill or concept taught.

Use mini-plenaries throughout the session to check pupils' progress, remind them of success criteria, instructions etc. and respond to any misconceptions. Don't wait until the end of the lesson to find out what they have or have not achieved.

### *Teaching*

- Explain the learning objective; link to prior learning where appropriate and/or something they already know, can do, have seen.
- Show students what a good one looks like (WAGOLL), what is possible.
- Show them how to achieve it (key teaching points/demonstration).
- Allow them time and opportunity to experience, explore and learn for themselves (time to practice and make mistakes or refine).
- Ensure time at the end for reflection and evaluation (making sense of it, assessing their own achievement, understanding what they need to do next).
- Make a note (mental or written) to inform your planning for the next session.

(Appendices 5–8 provide ideas for planning with clear objectives.)

## Designing activities

The Inclusion Spectrum, initially developed by Joseph Winnick, Professor of Physical Education at Brockport College in the USA, in his book *Adapted PE and Sport,* and first published in 1982, was adapted for UK educators in 1997 by the Youth Sport Trust, Liverpool Community College and the British Paralympic Association. It consists of five approaches to the delivery of PE and sport, each seeking to engage both disabled and non-disabled pupils.

**Open activities** get the whole group involved straight away, where the person's disability does not restrict what they're doing, for instance deaf athletes running with hearing athletes. Here everyone can achieve a degree of success.

In **modified activities** everyone has the same learning focus but accesses the learning in different ways, with changes to either the rules, the area played in or the equipment used. For instance, during a net and wall games session, a young disabled person may be practising their skills using a balloon and a lightweight racket alongside others using more traditional equipment. A person with mobility impairments playing tennis might be allowed an extra bounce.

**Parallel activities** are where everyone plays the same game, but different groups play in different ways and at different levels. For instance, tee ball may be played alongside rounders, with the teacher or coach focusing on the same rules, skills or tactics.

**Separate activities** give pupils the option of working on a totally different activity from the rest of the group. Individuals are grouped according to specific criteria, whether that's skill, fitness or the way they play.

These approaches can be included as part of the curriculum for everyone.

> Children have their own ways of making sure games are fair for everyone, know how to adapt and change. Modify things when necessary.
>
> Anne Craddock, SEND PE consultant

Photo: Simon Harris

## Gateway activities

Gateway activities give young people the chance to have a go at the sport at a basic level and have some fun, without too many expectations or pressures of how well they'll do, compared to their peers. The idea is to help someone enjoy their first experience of being active, to build confidence which will encourage the person to take part again.

For this approach to succeed, all involved – SEND pupils, peers, coach/teacher – must have appropriate expectations. The key is for the teacher or coach to focus on all participants as individuals, not to think they have twenty-five able-bodied players and four disabled players who need something different. The good teacher will target the activity at the needs and skill levels of all their players, giving all participants the chance to accomplish something on their own terms.

A series of fun, adventure-based tasks might enable children to experience failure as well as success, while also helping them to learn to work together. Alternatively, activities could focus on initiative, trust, communication, reflection, social responsibility, respect and positive leadership.

In 'Spider's Web', for example, groups of youngsters design ways of getting all their members inside a structure which looks a bit like a tent without the canvas. Each pupil has to get in through a different gap in the structure, which would then be flagged and not available for subsequent use. In this activity, no one can be left out. Everyone has to contribute, asking themselves such things as 'What order should we go in?', 'Who will need assistance to get through?' and 'Which person fits which gap the best?'

In 'Swamp of Death', mats become stepping stones in a scenario-based activity where students have to get across the swamp – in other words, their school hall or playground. One step in the swamp means the end for the whole group. The number of stones, each just big enough to get two feet on, should be considerably smaller than the number of people in the group. And don't forget a stone will float only while someone is in contact with it: lose contact and the stone will sink to the bottom of the swamp forever.

Again, this game requires teamwork. Youngsters, many of whom might have had a natural tendency to rush out alone, have to think of their contribution to the whole group rather than just themselves. In another activity, one child verbally assists blindfolded partners through a minefield of their own problems.

'Zoning' is an invasion game. Divide the pitch into three areas within which certain players must stay during any one passage of play. In the end zones, pupils have the ball at their feet and pass, tackle and move in the conventional way. In the middle zone, players use a hand-held net on a stick to intercept the ball. This means that students using wheelchairs can engage with the learning without the possibility of collisions or other children being tripped by nets. Able-bodied pupils would switch between zones, taking up each role in turn.

'Zone Hockey' integrates ambulant and mobility-impaired players into the same game. The pitch is divided into three longitudinal zones, with goal areas at each end and a goal, two metres across and one metre high. The central zone represents 50 per cent of the playing area and the two wing zones 25 per cent each. Players matched by needs and ability must stay within their own zone at all times. Safety dictates no physical contact and that sticks, even light plastic ones, must not be lifted above waist height.

Playing Zone Hockey enables young people to get the same benefits as if they were playing mini-hockey; they learn to control the ball, shoot from a still position (seated or standing) or on the move, as well as to pass to a target or partner. Using the zones helps them increase their spatial awareness. There's a lot of decision-making too. Pupils have to decide whether to control the ball before making a pass or shot or to stroke the ball first time; they have to select the correct weight of pass before playing a pass into the path of a moving teammate. They decide when to pass or when to shoot or when to communicate with teammates to keep possession.

> Most teachers and coaches have the skills and knowledge to include young people with special educational needs. The barriers are most often in their own heads, with people being afraid to make a mistake or ask a child to do something the child can't do. It just requires a little bit of flexibility and confidence.
>
> To make things simple, have as few rules as possible. So with cricket, there is no insistence on over-arm bowling, extra runs are given for hitting a ball against a wall – or for those with severe disabilities, simply hitting the ball. Youngsters who have problems gripping the plastic bat hard enough use tennis rackets – the strings providing extra impetus to their shots.
>
> To make activities more inclusive, let players hit the ball from a stationary position or allow them to throw underarm. Reduce the distance that children with mobility problems have to travel or perhaps have them score in ways that don't require travelling – maybe by taking a series of catches fed to them by a teammate as the ball is fielded. All of these strategies can be incorporated into a game or activity without altering the nature of the activity for the other children involved.
>
> Ian Martin, Head of Disability Cricket,
> England and Wales Cricket Board

Think 'people' rather than 'sport' and it's easier to be inclusive. Deliver lessons with predetermined sport-centred outcomes in mind and it will be more difficult to teach sport inclusively. If coaches believe that they have to pitch their sessions at a certain level in order to make these people good cricketers, footballers or hockey players, the sessions will be harder to access for those people, disabled or non-disabled, who are never going to be able to perform in the required way.

The best coaches and teachers start with the person and think: 'What do I need to do to help this person achieve what they want to achieve from my session?' Whether that is to reach their potential, get fitter, be part of a team, meet people or just enjoy themselves. The teacher or coach says to themselves: 'How am I going to get this person enthused and moving towards their personal goal?' And from this starting point, they can implement some of the strategies mentioned above, to help the person progress at the speed and in the direction most suited to that particular individual.

Sports coach UK publishes a guide to inclusive coaching which echoes this sentiment: 'Focus on what people can do rather than what they can't.' The guide explains that some disabled people need little, if any, change to the activities they do and the way they're taught or coached. Others require specific modifications to the space they play in, the tasks they do, the equipment they use, the number of people they play with and the speed at which they play. Sports coach UK uses the acronym STEPS to remind coaches and teachers of the variables at their disposal:

- space;
- tasks;
- equipment;
- people;
- speed.

Different pupils will need different adaptations of course. A person with a physical disability might need a bigger goal, target or net to aim at, or a shorter, lighter racket. Large coloured markers would help someone with learning difficulties understand where the playing area starts and finishes. Visual cues are essential for people with social difficulties and hearing impairments, and using the same space for each activity will help a person with a visual impairment.

## The inclusive teacher

Rather than take centre stage as the fount of all knowledge, the inclusive teacher is a guide or enabler. They make critical interventions, impart information and give useful feedback. Instead of barking out instructions from the front or centre, the inclusive PE teacher spends more time talking with individuals or small groups. This could be giving praise or encouragement, reinforcing learning goals, helping with misunderstandings or supporting pupils to overcome difficulties.

Some pupils respond better to questions; then they can work out for themselves what they need to do. 'Why were you unable to hold that position for more than a few seconds?' Others, though, will feel challenged by this tactic and perceive it as an attack on their efforts. These pupils might be engaged more effectively by a demonstration of a similar mistake, where it is not they who have done wrong in the eyes of their peers. Some will need to visualise a technique, whereas others will need to gain a greater understanding of what the technique is about or its short-term or long-term purpose, in order to progress.

Two young people are both having trouble connecting cleanly with the ball because they are playing their shots too early. Demonstrating the shot to the first youngster, or showing to the second, exactly where the ball must get to before they hit could facilitate greater progress. It may well be that a third child, in their eagerness not to make a mistake, is moving into position the second that they see the ball released from the sender's racket or hand. A critical intervention for this youngster would be to help them to relax, back their own judgement on when to move and not to fret about making a mistake.

Here, the teacher is helping pupils to see what it is they are aiming for and is raising their awareness and understanding of exactly what they need to do to improve.

Questions such as 'What do you need to do next?' or 'How can you achieve that?' will get pupils to think about what they're doing currently, and what might need altering or adapting in order to progress. If we ask, 'What is preventing you from achieving that goal?' or 'What happens if you are distracted by the group next to you?', we will help them to think about how to minimise negative effects. Finally, asking youngsters to consider how they know whether they have done well will enable them to realise that making progress is more than about just winning or being the best in the class. Questions like these are related to process rather than content and help young people develop their own learning strategies.

*The following advice is aimed at teachers involved with students who have Down's syndrome, but the guidance is useful for working with many learners who have SEND.*

**Be in close proximity** to the young person when you're talking to the class. If you just stop and shout across the playing area, the young person might not be able to hear you, particularly if there is some background noise, or if you are in a sports hall that echoes. Some children with Down's syndrome will need to lip read to understand you. So, call the group in, or if you don't want to stop, stand close by the young person with Down's syndrome when you speak to the group.

Children with Down's syndrome work well with **regularity, routine, repetition**. They can struggle if the location, time or teacher in charge changes. If there's to be a change, let the young person know in advance. Let them know in advance what is happening in the lesson. Children with Down's syndrome need repetition in lesson content, too, and one thing at a time, not too much crammed into one lesson. So if the skill focus of the lesson is running with the ball and passing, let them focus on just one of these areas.

**Keep instructions short and precise**; show the children what you want them to do rather than what you want them to achieve – for instance, 'Tap the ball with your foot around these cones to the tall marker' rather than 'Get the ball to the marker'. With the second instruction, some kids might just pick the ball up and walk over to the marker. Have a back-up plan in case something doesn't work.

Sophia Pittounikos, DS Active Officer
and coach, Down's Syndrome Association

Use plain English, not metaphor, adjectival buzz words, slang and sarcasm. I spoke to one young person who didn't know that 'brisk walking' meant walk faster.

Anne Craddock, SEND PE consultant

(See the eResources at www.routledge/9781138209015 for details of adapted activities: Polybat; Table Cricket; Target Cricket; Zone Hockey; Floor Lacrosse.)

## Inclusive dance

All pupils can be enabled to appreciate dance and respond to it in some way. Most can also participate at some level; for example, those with minimal movement can use their head, shoulders, mouth and face; power-chair users can use joysticks or switches. Many young people with SEND can explore ways to choreograph a dance sequence, focus their awareness of body movements and develop an understanding of shape and levels.

*Success for All* (2003), produced by the DfES and the English Federation of Disability Sport, the Youth Sport Trust and Inclusion, provides useful tips for teaching inclusive dance.

- Use a range of sounds, such as percussion, pop music, music from other cultures.
- Use a variety of apparatus, such as balloons, ribbons, material, bubbles, scarves or hoops.
- Develop pupils as choreographers. Give them a sound structure and let them develop the detail.
- Adapt movement, concentrating on what a pupil can do rather than what they can't; so if they can't use one side of the body, encourage them to use the other or facilitate one side, or to use hands instead of feet.
- Aim for a mood rather than a complicated step pattern with some pupils.
- Use a pupil's aid as a prop or a focus.
- Move from concrete concepts to more abstract ones.
- Use repetitive patterns.
- Use visual and sound cues.
- Use particular pupils as visual cues for pupils to follow, move towards, finish behind or in front of. A pupil with learning difficulties might be set a task to mirror a non-disabled pupil's movement (or vice versa in a buddy system).
- Encourage some pupils to undertake certain movements through colour-coded prompts, e.g. red – stop, green – go, blue – move to the right.

The resource goes on to explain how pupils with learning disabilities may not be aware of abstract concepts such as 'elevate', 'spiral' or 'hover', until they have experienced them first-hand. Teachers can help some pupils to discover the meanings of words by demonstrating an appropriate movement. Some pupils may need to hold or feel objects, such as using a fan to re-create walking against the wind, or to see a picture or a video of an animal before trying to copy its movements. Teachers can encourage pupils to increase their movement vocabulary by asking them to try to name the movements they make. With pupils who have a visual impairment (VI), other strategies can be adopted:

- Use tactile imagery, such as 'the hot sun', 'a cool, gurgling river', or give physical clues, such as 'a pointed church spire'.
- Incorporate manual tracking. For example, a pupil with a VI can follow the path of a movement by placing their hand on the back of a sighted partner's

hand. This can then be repeated, with sighted pupils tracking their visually impaired partner's movement.

For pupils with a short attention span, different combinations of tactile, verbal, musical and visual stimuli can help them to focus on an activity. Pupils who have a hearing impairment can be included more fully in dance activities by appreciating the way that sound is created and used in the dance. Live instruments are easier for pupils to appreciate than recorded sound, as they can feel the resonance of a wind instrument, or they can touch a drum while it is played in different ways.

> Look for movement outcomes not just sporting outcomes. Also key life skills: listening, social skills, co-operation, team work, respect for each other.
>
> Anne Craddock, SEND PE consultant

A variety of resources and lesson plans to support and inspire your planning can be found on the TES website: www.tes.com/teaching-resources/hub/secondary/physical-education (accessed 24 April 2017).

# 4 Monitoring and assessment

If you have a class that includes young people with SEND, you first have to find out what everyone can do and then tailor activities to fit their learning needs.

> She tries hard and always has a smile on her face, but due to her lack of mobility Sunita is unable to take part in most team games, so we are unable to give an accurate assessment of what she can do. Although she is 'sport mad', we recommend that she prioritises academic study over PE, when choosing her GCSE options, next year.
>
> (End-of-year school report)
>
> Two months after this end-of-year report, Sunita took part in a swimathon at her club, to raise money for a local charity. She swam two miles. Her school didn't have a pool – so they didn't do swimming.

Assessment should be about discovering what a pupil can do, not highlighting what they cannot. It is about helping children understand what has enabled them to get to a certain point and identifying strategies by which they can progress further or, if required, in alternative directions.

Assessment should be:

- child centred;
- concerned with process as well as outcome;
- concerned with more than just performance and skills (e.g. feelings and attitude);
- part of an ongoing dialogue between teacher and student that informs future learning – and future teaching.

## Formative assessment

Throwing a group of Year 7 pupils into a rigorous, performance-based assessment programme in their first term is unlikely to give an accurate picture of what each individual can do, how they best do it and what they need to do to progress further.

For any number of personal, social or emotional reasons, many youngsters may simply not be able to do their best in their first few weeks at a new school. Some schools have overcome this problem by designing a transition curriculum. As well as providing initial formative assessment, activities tend to concentrate on engaging pupils, sharing information, establishing departmental expectations and introducing the school ethos. Some schools run them for a few weeks, others over the first term; in some cases, the transition curriculum runs for the entire first year after transfer from primary school.

Such a transition curriculum in PE could involve:

- teachers and coaches visiting feeder primary schools and delivering sessions of PE so that pupils in Y6 get to know PE staff at their secondary schools;
- ensuring that visits by Y6 pupils to secondary schools include a tour of the PE department and facilities, and perhaps an activity session as well;
- secondary pupils making a video of the PE and sports activities that take place in the secondary school, and sharing this with Y6/7 pupils;
- teaching pupils in Y7 in their former primary school groups, so they're not inhibited about performing in front of unfamiliar peers;
- collecting information from the pupils themselves about their interests and strengths in PE and sport, and any personal targets they may have;
- running 'basic skills' modules that focus on fundamental movements and techniques. Pupils can be given information about what they can expect to learn in each module – with space in a log book or folder to record their own achievements and their attitudes towards PE.

These activities provide a useful introduction to PE at secondary school and can give teachers and coaches valuable information to inform their decisions about grouping pupils.

## Assessment for learning

> The National Curriculum is more flexible than is often perceived. Often teachers look for instructions to inform their delivery, rather than focusing on what pupils have to achieve. It can be inclusive – it's just a question of interpretation.
>
> PE Consultant Crichton Casbon, formerly with the QCA

Assessment for learning (AfL) is about identifying an individual's needs and working out the best way to help them achieve their goals. It is less about keeping records and more to do with reflecting on options, establishing priorities and raising student awareness of what progress actually looks like.

It starts with questions. If everyone involved is asking questions about the learning that's going on, then teachers, other adults or leaders and, most crucially of all, pupils themselves will be involved in an ongoing process of observation and evaluation.

- What are you trying to achieve?
- How did you achieve it?
- What do we need to do to progress?
- Why did that go wrong?
- Is that task too easy or too hard at the moment?
- Are there other ways of doing that?
- Why did it go wrong that time and not the other time?

There are different types of questions to use in every lesson: closed functional questions, e.g. about rules and equipment etc., and more open questions which require choices or comparisons to be made, perhaps with some analysis and evaluation involved. The trick is using the appropriate question to prompt the response or action you want to elicit. Some youngsters will need to work out for themselves what they need to do to progress; others will be less independent and need prompting, or even showing.

We should also remember the importance of encouraging pupils to ask questions, not only of the teacher or coach but also of each other:

- How do you know where to stand?
- How do you decide who to pass to?
- When do you take a breath (swimming)?
- What do you think about when you serve?
- Where do you look when you try to serve, score, hit the ball?

This takes practice; many pupils with SEND struggle to think of any relevant question to ask. But both asking and answering questions can help develop understanding of what works in different situations, and what an individual can try to do to improve their skills.

Over time, if young people are encouraged to think for themselves (remember to give them some 'thinking time'), they will become more independent and learn more quickly.

## Assessment tasks

Assessment tasks provide a sense of focus to lessons and modules, allowing youngsters to piece together their short-term learning and build towards something bigger. Usually, young people need to learn or improve a whole range of skills and develop a range of knowledge to play a game or sport, or just to engage with a physical activity.

Often these individual concepts are learnt better in isolation, especially when pupils have learning difficulties: youngsters are able to focus on a specific set of requirements for a whole session. Organising modules around assessment tasks allows young people to learn these concepts and then gradually piece them together and relate them to the overall assessment objective. By concentrating on specific skills or concepts, we can provide clear success criteria – which can be different for different individuals – and involve pupils in self-assessment and peer assessment.

A teacher's ingenuity is called for in devising tasks which fulfil the need for practising and assessing specific skills and concepts. Fielding drills, for example, can be boring, but you need to learn how to perform these skills if you're going to play cricket, baseball, rounders and other striking and fielding games. In the lesson outlined below, pupils were motivated by an adapted 'invasion' game, where rewards were given for completing throws and catches, rather than scoring goals or baskets. The teacher asked questions at various points throughout the lesson, such as: 'How did you make sure you caught the ball? How and when would you use these skills during a game of rounders?' Teaching interventions took the form of questions related to catching and throwing techniques and also how to stop a ball that is rolling along the ground.

### A fielding lesson

Using a tennis ball, two teams of four scored points by hitting a target – a large cone – at the opposite end of a pitch which was divided into zones.

There was to be no moving whilst in possession of the ball, no physical contact and, on a small pitch, underarm throwing below head height only. To prevent defenders from standing in front of the target and making it impossible to hit, one group came up with the idea of setting up a small no-go area around the target.

Another group decided that teams would be rewarded with a point for every five consecutive catches that they made. A third decided that every member of the group must touch the ball prior to a point being scored, while a few students, not particularly fond of learning through competition, preferred to practise their throwing and catching skills in the traditional way, designing for themselves a series of tests to encourage progress. This kind of approach encourages pupils to think creatively about how to develop skills and tactics independently.

While practising stopping a moving ball, one pupil in a wheelchair used a chute to roll the ball along the ground to a partner and then positioned himself behind a long table, especially brought over from the school canteen, to receive the return. He couldn't bend down and pick the ball up off the ground, but he could stop a moving ball – which was the focus of the lesson. His partner, an able-bodied child, didn't lose out because the focus of the session was not to do with rolling a ball along the ground. The disabled youngster, who suffers from muscular dystrophy, lacked the strength to throw the ball in the air. But rearranging the pairs into a group of three meant that he could be included in the lesson. While his partners threw the ball in the air to each other, they took it in turns to continue rolling it to him. The group did try positioning the chute on the edge of the table and taking catches when the ball rolled off. One youngster in the school cricket team saw this going on and thought it would be an ideal way of practising slip catching.

## Target setting

Working towards assessment tasks enables both long and short-term targets to be set. To be inclusive, targets must be personalised and realistic – related to what the students themselves can do.

However, even at KS1, the national curriculum for PE talks of developing 'balance, agility and co-ordination'. Some pupils with SEND will never achieve this; even some national champions in disability sport would struggle. These youngsters can, however, often improve on their existing levels of control and co-ordination. An inclusive approach would assess an individual according to, and based on, an awareness of their own unique needs. Take the earlier example of the pupil in a wheelchair who can stop a moving ball. Does it say anywhere that the ball has to be travelling along the ground? If the sport-centric argument is used that in cricket, baseball and rounders the ball will travel along the floor, the solution for severely disabled youngsters may be in Table Cricket (see the eResources at www.routledge.com/9781138209015) and so their PE experience is equally relevant.

Staff in the PE department also have to bear in mind the personal targets assigned to an individual as part of a support plan or pupil passport. There will usually be literacy and numeracy targets, and PE lessons can contribute in a very practical way to helping pupils develop in these areas. Literacy development might include: reading out rules, writing up a match report, learning new vocabulary; numeracy might be practised by keeping/collating scores, measuring speed and distance, timing races, etc. All such activities are afforded more meaning when applied to PE and sport rather than practised as paper exercises in the classroom and, as such, can be very much more motivating to pupils.

Individual plans may also describe generic aims which can be worked on very effectively in PE, with staff recording and reporting on a pupil's progress, for example:

- improving social skills (working in a pair or a team; turn-taking; accepting defeat; playing by the rules);
- developing listening skills (digesting rules and instructions; co-operating with classmates);
- developing spoken communication (working effectively with a partner, sharing a game plan, giving instruction, peer coaching);
- improving organisational skills (remembering to bring kit; choosing and organising a team; setting up equipment).

Pupils who find it difficult to behave appropriately in a classroom often demonstrate exemplary behavior in the gym or on the sports field; this is an opportunity for teachers and coaches to acknowledge and praise positive actions and, importantly, to share positive feedback with parents and other staff. Success and enjoyment in PE can be powerful in boosting self-esteem and confidence for pupils who struggle in academic subjects.

## Adapted targets

Rather than thinking of a skill in terms of its 'absolute mechanics', teachers can consider its application and how it relates to a pupil's physical and cognitive capabilities. In this way, more appropriate targets can be set, such as those listed in Figure 4.1.

## P scales

Where children are learning more slowly than their peers, it's particularly important to recognise and celebrate progress. P scales are broad descriptions that can be used to assess progress in the PE curriculum for pupils who are not yet achieving in line with age-related expectations (see Figure 4.2). They allow for the evaluation of an individual's progress and provide a clear indication of their development.

| A pupil can: |
|---|
| **run and jump by**<br>• walking/running – travel slowly/quickly by wheeling, shuffling, crawling or stepping<br>• hopping – moving part of the body, arm, leg from one side to the other, or hopping with both feet together<br>• wheelchair users can use arms to lift body into the air as an alternative to jumping<br>• moving body over low objects, mat or beam<br>• extending and contracting all or part of the body<br>• wheelchair users can also travel as far as possible with one push (long jump) |
| **travel with a ball by**<br>• holding the ball in their arms<br>• clutching the ball against their body<br>• balancing the ball on their lap or other part of their body<br>• holding the ball in a receptacle<br>• pushing the ball along under control<br>• using equipment that is easier to hold (e.g. quoits, bean bags) |
| **send the ball by**<br>• rolling or pushing it along the floor<br>• using a channel, tube or gutter device<br>• rolling it at table-top level<br>• using hands, feet or any flat surface of the body (e.g. forearm)<br>• rolling it down the body from a seated position<br>• using part of a wheelchair, sticks, crutches, rollator<br>• using a channel on the floor or table top<br>• releasing it in the most effective (rather than technical) arm position |
| **send and receive by**<br>• rolling the ball against a wall<br>• rolling it along a table top pushed against the wall, or lap tray with a 'rebounder'<br>• having it rolled rather than bounced<br>• having time to control the ball or not having to send the ball in one movement |
| **receive a ball by**<br>• stopping it with a part of the body, wheelchair, crutch, stick, rollator<br>• gathering the ball into the body using arms, legs or an implement<br>• gathering and controlling the ball using an enclosed space (e.g. corner)<br>• retrieving it using a string attached to the chair, wheelchair, racket<br>• having the ball replaced by a softer implement, e.g. a bean bag, koosh ball, partially deflated ball, no-bounce ball, spider ball |
| **kick a ball from a stationary position or while on the move by**<br>• using a slower or faster moving ball<br>• kicking from a seated position<br>• using a crutch, stick or rollator to strike the ball<br>• using a partially deflated ball or bean bag for greater control |
| **strike a ball**<br>• with a bigger/smaller bat (larger or smaller striking area)<br>• by using a bigger/smaller ball (easier/harder to hit)<br>• from a stationary position on a T or cone<br>• using a rolled, bounced, delivery feed<br>• using a hand or forearm to strike<br>• using a bat glove or bat/racket attached to hand or arm |

*Figure 4.1* Enabling strategies

The P scales describe achievements in PE and can be useful as 'performance descriptors' for students with SEND. The performance descriptors for P1–P3 are the same across the curriculum; P4–P8 are tailored for individual subjects and those for PE are listed below.

| | |
|---|---|
| **P4** | • Pupils' movement patterns are established and they perform single actions [for example, rolling, running, jumping or splashing]<br>• They respond to simple commands [for example, 'stop']<br>• They recognise familiar pieces of equipment [for example, a ball or hoop]<br>• They show awareness of cause and effect [for example, knocking down skittles]. |
| **P5** | • Pupils link two actions in a sequence [for example, crawling and walking, or climbing and jumping]<br>• They follow simple instructions although they may need the support of symbols or other prompts<br>• They explore a variety of movements and show some awareness of space<br>• They understand some basic concepts [for example, taking big and little steps in movement activities or placing big and small balls in different baskets]<br>• They take turns with a partner or in a small group<br>• They recognise and collect, on request, familiar pieces of equipment [for example, a mat to lie on or a hoop to jump into]. |
| **P6** | • Pupils work in pairs and in small groups cooperatively, although they may need support to follow instructions and keep on task<br>• They move in a variety of ways [for example, slowly and quickly]<br>• They link movements in a simple sequence, although they may require support to do this<br>• They recognise small and large apparatus and use it with some basic control<br>• They throw and kick a ball, but lack direction. |
| **P7** | • Pupils express themselves through repetitive and simple sequences and movement patterns<br>• Their control and coordination skills are developing [for example, they kick a ball towards a target or throw a ball to a partner]<br>• They listen to instructions and stop and start with some accuracy<br>• They work closely in pairs, trios or small groups<br>• They share and wait their turn<br>• They are aware of the changes that happen to their bodies when they are active. |
| **P8** | • Pupils move with some control and coordination [for example, they travel under and over climbing equipment]<br>• They follow and imitate sequences and patterns in their movements<br>• They use small and large apparatus safely<br>• They are aware of space, themselves and others<br>• They play simple games and may require support to keep score and follow game rules<br>• They recognise the changes that happen to their bodies when they are active. |

*Figure 4.2* P scales for PE (as outlined by the DfE in 2014)

www.gov.uk/government/uploads/system/uploads/attachment_data/file/329911/Performance_-_P_Scale_-_attainment_targets_for_pupils_with_special_educational_needs.pdf

P scales outline early learning and attainment in PE and can be used by teachers to:

- decide which description best fits a pupil's performance over a period of time and in different contexts;
- develop or support more focused day-to-day approaches to ongoing teacher assessment by using the descriptions to refine and develop long, medium and short-term planning;

- track linear progress towards age-related expectations;
- identify lateral progress by looking for related skills at similar levels across their subjects;
- record pupils' overall development and achievement, for example at the end of a year or a key stage.

Photo: Simon Harris

## What is progress?

Assessment in PE should be more than a measurement of performance; it should also include an evaluation of the effect it has on pupils' mental health and wellbeing. Even the most hard-nosed, back-to-basics government minister might recognise that if students are going to achieve, or better still surpass, their potential academically, they need to be in good health, physically and mentally. Even the most results-driven head teacher might see that a young person's work will suffer if they are stressed, overweight, inactive and generally unhappy.

Youngsters are under more pressure than ever before to succeed at school. They know that how well they do in tests and exams will determine their future: whether they go to university, find employment, enjoy fulfilling careers. Some say that these young people have more stress but less access to support than previous cohorts.

Sport and physical activity can play a part here. Sport and exercise help people feel better – about themselves and about life in general. In November 2014 Public Health England, the government's health watchdog, released a report that linked young people's health and academic attainment to the amount of physical activity they do. The report linked the intensity and duration of children's exercise to their academic performance. Researchers also stated that youngsters who do more physical activity behave better in class, get on with their peers and are less likely to disrupt lessons. Participation in extra-curricular activities was also seen to have a positive effect on attainment: pupils engaged in self-development activities, including sport and physical activity, achieved 10–20 per cent higher in their GCSEs.

An earlier study in the *British Journal of Sports Medicine* identified that the amount of moderate to vigorous physical activity pupils engaged with at age 11 had an effect on academic performance across English, maths and science. This was also found to be the case during their final GCSE exams. Between 2007 and 2010 the number of sports college students achieving five A*–C grades increased by 7.8 per cent (the national average increase was 4 per cent). This study also stated that the more time girls spent in moderate to vigorous physical activity at age 11, the better their predicted science scores at 11 and 16.

(See Appendix 9 for a checklist to use with individual students in evaluating their involvement and achievement in PE and sport.)

# 5 Sport, exercise and mental health

Department of Health figures show that one in four people in the UK will suffer from mental health problems during their lifetime, and one in six people at any given time. That's anxiety, addiction, obsession, phobia, depression, bipolar disorder, personality disorder, schizophrenia, eating disorders. The consequences of ignoring young people's mental wellbeing can be grave indeed. According to the Youth Sport Trust, there are 850,000 5–16 year olds in the UK with a diagnosable mental illness. This manifests in bullying, cyber bullying, self-harm.

In an average class of thirty 15-year-old pupils:

- three could have a mental disorder
- ten are likely to have witnessed their parents separate
- one could have experienced the death of a parent
- seven are likely to have been bullied
- six may be self-harming

'Promoting children and young people's emotional health and wellbeing A whole school and college approach', www.gov.uk/government/uploads/system/uploads/attachment_data/file/414908/Final_EHWB_draft_20_03_15.pdf (accessed 6 February 2017)

According to mental health charity Mind, research shows that outdoor exercise can reduce depression and anxiety, by up to 30 per cent according to the Youth Sport Trust. Physical activity gets the endorphins going and can lift a person's mood almost immediately. Just being outdoors can help. There's light, you're surrounded by nature, away from those more bustling environments which may hold negative associations.

The Mental Health Foundation says that exercise releases chemicals in the brain that make people feel good. 'Regular exercise can also boost your self-esteem, improve your confidence and help you concentrate, sleep, look and feel better', a charity spokesperson said. 'It can help you feel valued – and value yourself.' The foundation believes that short bursts of regular exercise help people in many ways. Regular exercise reduces tension, stress and mental fatigue, provides a natural energy boost and improves sleep. It can also engender a sense of achievement, provide a focus in life and some motivation. People who exercise regularly feel less angry and frustrated and are more likely to have a healthy appetite and a better social life. And on top of all that, playing sport can be a lot of fun.

Playing sport provides exercise, but it also has additional benefits. Rules and conventions govern play. Pupils perform as individuals and as part of a team. They learn, apply and develop skills, knowledge and strategies. Structured activity requires participants to think about what's going on around them and to focus; there's no time to think about their problems. They can learn to ignore external distractions, concentrate on the task at hand and work towards short-term, individual targets. With teammates, pupils also work towards longer-term targets. By taking action and shutting out negative external and internal influences, they can begin moulding their future by reacting to everyday occurrences in a way that brings them what they want.

## Therapeutic sport

A sports session for a young person with mental health issues is not about training to become part of a team or promoting a sport to them; nor is it necessarily about learning skills and improving performance. That sort of session creates pressure to do well, to be better than someone else, and to win. For young people with mental health issues that means more stress and anxiety. A *therapeutic* sports session aims to ensure that the young person will come back to the next session, so they can continue to benefit from the activity and build up their self-esteem. The young person needs to feel welcome, however good they are at sport.

The activity is supposed to make people feel better, so you don't want the coach or teacher shouting at them to do that little bit extra. The coach needs to have a secure understanding of why students are there, and what they need. Young people with mental health issues need consistent delivery. Ideally, that's an extended warm-up, some skills work based on individual success, rather than comparative or performance-based criteria, and some small-sided games. Again, you start with what the person can do, rather than what they can't.

It's also important for the teacher or coach to be aware of the effect a pupil's issues might have on the individuals they are working with. That doesn't mean an in-depth knowledge of the ins and outs of every person's life, or a medical practitioner's knowledge of various conditions. An awareness that people will occasionally have a bad day is useful though, and that their state of mind will influence how they behave during the session. Medication affects different people in different ways: some might be hyperactive, others might need a break from time to time. A lot of young people with mental health issues have poor body image, are self-harming or suffer from depression.

All PE teachers and coaches need enough knowledge and understanding to ensure that they aren't out of their depth if such matters arise in conversation, or if they observe something indicating a potentially difficult situation. It is crucial that they can signpost pupils to the sort of help they need.

> The main challenge for schools is to provide the right sporting and physical activity offer. One that encourages as many children as possible to get involved and stay involved, so they can feel the benefit. While curriculum time PE is essential for developing children's fundamental movement skills, children must have access to a wide range of sport and physical activity opportunities outside of formal PE — before, during and after school.
>
> Ideally there would be enough time on the curriculum for teachers to design a curriculum that all young people want to take part in. This would give children the opportunity to gain all the benefits. At primary school kids tend to take up lots of different activities. At secondary school, when they start making choices about their path, they'll opt out of sport if they don't think it's relevant to their chosen lifestyle.
>
> Many young people don't play sport to compete or to improve their skills. They take part to be with friends, to connect with others and to feel part of something. Traditionally there has been too much emphasis on teaching skills required to play sports. There needs to be more focus on what young people are learning through playing sport. That's how PE and sport teaching will adapt to modern times, become relevant to today's young people.
>
> Chris Wright, Head of Health and Wellbeing, Youth Sport Trust

## Getting the balance right

The trick is to get the balance right between teaching sports skills and physical literacy and promoting the wider benefits of PE and sport. It's possible to fit into lessons advice about the way PE and sport can help young people in other areas of their life. Maybe an extra hour a week on the PE timetable where teachers focus on just this would work. This would help young people understand the links between sport, an active lifestyle and their overall wellbeing.

Teaching this sort of thing more explicitly might encourage more reluctant participants to see value in getting involved. Teachers sell the value of their subject to young people, but with sport you also have to reach out to parents. If parents see no value in PE and sport, then they'll just write their child a sick note every time he or she doesn't feel like taking part.

With government and schools increasingly focused on academic attainment and standards, PE and sport could play more of a supporting role in schools over the coming years. Its relevance might be determined more by how it helps individuals achieve better and more fulfilling lives than by how many young people take part, how many matches school teams win and how many elite athletes are produced.

This is in accordance with the Department for Culture, Media and Sport's strategy, announced in December 2015. At grass-roots level, DCMS says that it is looking to focus on projects that have a meaningful, measurable impact on improving people's lives; that could be helping young people gain skills they need for work, tackling social inclusion or improving mental health.

The latest Youth Sport Trust strategy also encourages schools to use sport to help young people live better lives and live in better communities. If you don't have physical and emotional health and wellbeing right, it doesn't matter what you do, young people will not achieve.

> Sports provision targeted at health and wellbeing needs would not just help students with diagnosable mental health issues, or people from poorer communities. It could also be talented, high achieving students who have a high level of expectation around them, either from parents, teachers and peers, who suffer from mental health problems.
>
> Schools need to redefine the purpose of PE and sport, working out how best to use it to teach life skills. For school leadership this is a cultural issue, to do with the emphasis schools place on the role of PE and the time they give to it. Schools are under pressure to devote more of their time, and their pupils' time, to academia and testing. This determines how staff are performance managed and how schools are funded.
>
> Chris Wright, Head of Health and Wellbeing, Youth Sport Trust

## Case study: cricket and mental health

Many high-profile cricketers have suffered from mental health issues in recent times. Somerset and former England batsman Marcus Trescothick first experienced depression when he was away from home, on tour with the England team. Spin bowler Monty Panesar says his anxiety issues were brought on by loss of self-esteem and issues in his personal life. New Zealand fast bowler Iain O'Brien battled depression throughout his career. Australian quick Shaun Tait took time out from the game when injuries and the pressure of unfulfilled expectations got too much for him. Andrew Flintoff said his depression got better when he gave up drinking.

Sport at the highest level is about highs and lows and long periods away from home. It means pressure to perform and to maintain standards, a place in the team and a living. There's also expectation from teammates, bosses, fans and the media, not to mention fear of injury and anxiety about what to do after retirement. Cricket can actually be good for people's mental health, though, if players, teachers and coaches don't worry too much about how well everyone does or who wins.

Cricket is a team game, but there are lots of different individual roles for people of different abilities. These roles are clearly defined and require discipline. If young people take turns to captain their team, they learn how to organise others, lead and take responsibility. This helps them to build self-confidence and to start doing things with their life again.

Some people on medication struggle with their fitness during faster-moving games, whereas cricket can be played at a slower pace and you don't have to run around all the time. It's a non-contact sport that can be played with a soft-ball, if necessary. Cricket also teaches target setting, focus, co-operation, preparation and other social skills.

West Indian cricketer Chris Gayle and a UK cricket charity, Cricket 4 Change, run projects for disadvantaged youngsters in Croydon and in Kingston, Jamaica. The Change Foundation is another charity that uses sport to help young people change their lives. Their programmes, however, are all about the individuals themselves and provide opportunities for young people to learn about and play sport, but also to equip them for life by building their confidence and helping them access the skills and training they need to go back into their communities and achieve their potential.

The foundation runs a cricket academy for 16–24 year olds, fronted by Gayle, who visits the young people occasionally and offers advice via video chat from his home in Jamaica. Some of these young people are excluded from school, others are former offenders. There are gang members and Afghan refugees on the project, all of them young people struggling to find their way in life, who without assistance might never fulfil their true potential.

During their first year at the academy, the youngsters work with coaches on a personal development plan that aims to help them become more employable. They get visits from local employers and careers advisers, who talk to the young people about job hunting, CVs, courses and aspirations. They also take a cricket coaching course and, in year two, will coach their own community teams.

When they play games of cricket, coaches focus on how aspects of the game apply to wider life; decision-making, communication, leadership and co-operation take precedence over technique training. The young people thrive on the responsibility afforded them. As practice matches play out on Cricket 4 Change's Plough Lane cricket ground, the youngsters take time for a laugh and a joke, chilling out while they're waiting to bat and engaging each other with a bit of good-natured banter. When the game starts, however, they're watching, thinking, making decisions about how best to get the upper hand.

Through cricket, young people learn discipline, responsibility and how to set goals. Staff use what happens in the games to show players the consequences of their actions, and how what they do affects others.

## Chris Gayle's 'big six' philosophy

Six things to do to ensure success on the cricket field and off it:

1. **Make good choices.** The decisions you make will affect how you handle a situation.
2. **Understand consequences and actions.** Things don't always happen how you want them to. You find ways to cope and it makes you stronger, more determined to succeed and overcome obstacles.
3. **Work hard.** Allow setbacks to make you more determined. Let difficulties drive you on, and more often than not you'll be able to take advantage of the opportunities put in front of you.
4. **Set goals.** Break down what you have to do to reach your target.
5. **Look after yourself.** Get enough sleep before a big day. If you are out until late, make sure you make up for it by sleeping more the next day.
6. **Respect other team members.** People might not be as talented as you, but they still have to perform well for the team to succeed. Understand their strengths and weaknesses and how they fit with your own, as part of the team.

## Case study: dance and mental health

In 2013 Anna Duberg, a physical therapist at Orebo University Hospital in Sweden, found that dance helped adolescent girls suffering from depression and poor self-image feel better about themselves.

Girls aged 13 to 18 took twice weekly jazz, African and contemporary dance classes over an eight-month period. Some forty-three out of forty-eight girls said they felt better after the classes. Researchers also found that this effect lasted for between four and eight months after the dance programme had finished.

> Dance gives people the benefits of exercise and social activity. But unlike in certain sports, you don't compete with others for points and you're not judged on how well you do.
>
> Anna Duberg

Duberg made sure the girls' dance lessons focused on the joy of movement rather than pushing them to improve their performance. It was dance for dance's sake; they weren't rehearsing for a show. The girls said that they enjoyed the lessons because they were undemanding. Many of them made new like-minded friends. They also chose some of the music and choreography themselves, took ownership of what they were doing, and as a result became more committed to it.

People with mental health issues get lots of benefits from dance. They can express how they feel, become more aware of their own emotions and explore different issues from the past in a safe environment. By changing their movements during a dance people can change how they feel and start to feel more positive.

Dance can be good for people who have negative feelings about their bodies such as an eating problem or body dysmorphic disorder, where a person has a distorted view, usually negative, of what their body looks like. Dance also works if someone has an emotional problem that comes out as a physical illness, which sometimes happens with depression. It's also good for people who find physical contact with other people difficult, and for those who feel detached or disconnected from their surroundings, or out-of-touch with everyday life. Some people with mental health issues take medication that affects the way they move, so dance is good for them, too.

Sam Challis, Mind

## Mental health sport training

Street Games are in discussions with the Paul Hamlyn Foundation about running mental health awareness training for workshops for sports coaches and volunteers, as part of the Right Here project: www.streetgames.org/bookings/contact-us/ (accessed 8 May 2017).

Royal Society for Public Health run a Level 1 in Health Improvement, which focuses on people's overall wellbeing, of which mental health is a part: https://www.rsph.org.uk (accessed 8 May 2017).

Mental Health First Aid England run a two-day mental health first aid course: http://mhfaengland.org/find-your-course (accessed 8 May 2017).

Mind are planning to set up mental health awareness training for coaches later this year. Local Mind offices will work with their county sports partnerships, local authorities and other local groups: www.mind.org.uk/ and www.copingthroughfootball.org/ (accessed 8 May 2017).

# 6 Accessing and managing support

For most teachers, the concept of support for pupils with SEND is synonymous with the deployment of teaching assistants (TAs) or support/curriculum/inclusion assistants (schools have developed a range of titles for this part of the workforce). In terms of PE and sport provision, however, there is a much larger net to be cast, and teachers should be well-informed about the support, funding and opportunities available for improving youngsters' access to activities.

## Teaching assistants

The trend for employing an ever-increasing number of TAs, coupled with a tendency for teachers to rely on them for 'taking care' of pupils with SEND, have, however, been stemmed by recently published research. Starting with the DISS study (Deployment and Impact of Support Staff: 2003–8 – Blatchford *et al*. 2009), researchers have found that TA involvement has often shown no evidence at all of improving outcomes for students; in fact in some cases there has been a negative effect. Subsequent projects, e.g. the 'Effective Deployment of Teaching Assistants', have made a convincing argument for schools to reassess how they recruit, train and deploy these paraprofessionals. With the right sort of knowledge, experience and attitude, TAs can play a major role in meeting students' individual needs and maximising their potential. Alternatively, and there are plenty of examples to illustrate this, a misguided, albeit well-meaning, TA can nurture dependency in a child, act as a barrier between him/her and the qualified teacher or coach, and significantly limit the pupil's learning and progress; the case study of Kerri is an illuminating example of such an instance.

## Case study: Kerri, a girl with moderate learning difficulties

Kerri was in tears after her first PE lesson at secondary school. Her class had been given a striking and fielding task to do, which was used as a formative assessment of everyone's initial capabilities in that subject area. But Kerri had hated every second of it. She was adamant that she was never doing PE again. In fact, it took several hours of persuading from her parents that evening before she was even prepared to come to school the next day.

It transpired that, at her primary school, Kerri had been allowed to opt out of PE whenever she felt like it. So when, during the aforementioned lesson, she had been asked to take part in a small-sided game, independently, she simply couldn't cope. At primary school she only had to look sad or, if that didn't work, cry and a sympathetic adult would take her to one side to find out what was the matter – quite a cunning avoidance strategy. What was the point of listening to and following instructions, when you only had to pull a face and someone would come and tell you what to do again?

When her new PE teacher spoke to her before her next PE lesson, she discovered that the last time Kerri had played a similar striking game was at primary school. When it was her turn to bat, the class TA had stood alongside her, helping her hold the bat. As the ball came down, they swung the bat together: 'There you go! Well done.' And this was an able-bodied child with moderate learning difficulties who would be quite capable of taking part.

As the module progressed, strategies to increase the students' independence were introduced. For Kerri, this had to be done gradually. Her levels of self-confidence regarding her own capacity to achieve anything independently were very low. Kerri was part of a group who initially struck the ball from a T, rather than having it fed to them by a teammate or, in the case of the more able group, an opponent. She liked the fact that she was not the only one to be hitting the ball in this way and that the targets set for each group weren't shared with the other group. She didn't like to stand out or let others realise she wasn't as good as them.

Kerri also enjoyed the activity cards her group was given, which had diagrams to remind her what she had to do. Slowly, Kerri began to improve her skills. She found that asking her teammates to roll, rather than throw, the ball to her made it easier for her to stop the ball, when fielding. By the end of the module she was able to strike a moving ball with some consistency.

Kerri still wouldn't class PE as her favourite subject, and she still doesn't attend any after-school or lunchtime clubs. However, she doesn't try to get out of doing it anymore; there are no tears and, now that she has realised that she can do things for herself, she can be quite spiky towards the unsuspecting teacher or TA who offers her advice, when she appears to be struggling.

'I actually can do it, you know!'

TAs employed to support individual pupils (usually those who have significant needs and therefore often an EHC plan) will know the child very well and will be a useful source of information about exactly what the pupil can and cannot do and, hopefully, an ally if the child needs persuading to have a go at new activities.

TAs can also

- encourage pupils to remain focused and on task;
- reduce the incidence of disruptive behaviour;
- foster greater pupil independence;
- increase pupils' confidence and self-esteem;
- raise attainment.

Staff in the PE department may give TAs more specific roles, such as:

- clarifying and explaining instructions, questions, tasks;
- keeping pupils on task;
- overseeing the setting up and care of equipment;
- reading or helping pupils to read written material;
- assisting pupils in practice;
- monitoring pupil behaviour;
- differentiating tasks and equipment;
- encouraging and praising pupils;
- helping pupils to work towards their individual targets;
- keeping teachers informed of difficulties encountered by pupils;
- suggesting to the teacher ways in which pupils could access the PE curriculum more easily;
- developing positive relationships with pupils;
- contributing information about pupils' progress.

Specialist PE teaching assistants could be a great asset. Specialists with a knowledge of PE and understanding of SEND issues – sports coaches, or even other adults with an interest in sport or simply a playing background – could be trained as PE-specific TAs. PE staff and coaches could provide subject-specific training.

As well as supporting individual children within lessons and liaising with the SEND department, such individuals, especially if they were given flexible working hours, could be involved in:

- leadership, coaching and officiating in after-school clubs and matches;
- collating information about pupil participation and progress; this could involve responsibility for producing interactive displays to assist and inform learning;
- administration of bookings, courses, fixtures and travel;
- liaising with outside organisations.

It's important to think beyond the confines of the school and what the personnel of the PE department have the time for – instead, consider:

- What sort of sport, physical activity and PE best suits a young person's needs?
- What can PE staff not deliver and how can we effectively access a range of partners and structures to fill any gaps in provision?
- Who, locally, are the best partners? Special schools, sports clubs, community groups, disability experts?
- Who within the school will be responsible for co-ordinating support networks?
- How can we help pupils with SEND use facilities which may involve travel beyond the local area?

Accessing activities outside school is not always straightforward for young people with SEND. A survey commissioned by Parallel London (2015) – organisers of a day of mass-participation running and walking events in London – found that 80 per cent of people with a disability still feel prejudice when participating in sport and leisure activities. Some 69 per cent of respondents said they faced barriers in accessing fitness and leisure facilities. Almost all said they would be more active if barriers and prejudices were removed.

There are sporting opportunities out there: some are designed for people with a specific disability, while others exist within mainstream settings where organisers have made arrangements to include disabled people. There are many disabled young people who would like to have a go at these activities, but often the problem is bringing people and opportunity together. Left to their own devices, some young people with SEND might not even think about playing sport, let alone find a place to play, get themselves there and stick at it, once they've started a new activity. In many cases, youngsters do not realise the extent and variety of sports sessions on offer.

Similarly, sports and physical activity professionals who run the programmes don't always know where the potential participants are or, even if they do, how best to get them to the activity setting. Sometimes people running things don't know how to meet a person's needs.

There's a role here for a teacher or a support worker who has weekly or even daily access to the young people. There are youngsters who want to take part and providers who need participants for their activities. It's a no-brainer that schools, who have the young people but not always the expertise, could act to bring the two together, encourage young people to take part, give organisations access. This is another way in which teachers and support workers can be absolutely crucial in helping people with learning and/or physical disabilities make a decision to lead an active lifestyle.

To find out where the activity is, locally, call the local authority and the nearest County Sports Partnership. County Sports Partnerships are local networks of groups and individuals involved in grass-root sport and physical activity. They have dedicated staff responsible for different areas of provision. Ask to speak to their disability lead. This person will have all the information you need about what is going on locally. Activities could be taking place in clubs, at universities, in community settings. This is the best way to find out exactly what is going on and where.

All national governing bodies of sport have equity targets, set for them by government through Sport England. This means that they need to secure and sustain the involvement in their chosen sport of more girls, youngsters from ethnic minority and disadvantaged backgrounds, and children with physical and learning disabilities. To keep the money coming from central government, they are also required to work with schools. Sports-specific programmes of activities, equipment and specially trained coaches are available for schools. It's just a case of finding them and making contact.

Understand each individual's needs and help them find the right activity. Speak to the young person about what they'd like to do. Do they find social situations difficult? Do they struggle with winning and losing? If so, maybe team sports such as football or basketball aren't quite right and they need something individual, maybe athletics or swimming – an activity where there's less risk of exposure to peers. Sometimes people need a bit of reassurance that the environment will be enjoyable and supportive. Many clubs and sports organisations have done a lot of work to make their activities inclusive.

### Agencies

Each region of England should have a dance development agency. These are organisations who receive public funding to deliver dance. Some will have a specialism in disability dance, but all will be able to point you in the direction of a group, locally, that does. Some will provide regular classes, others, special projects. **www.onedanceuk.org/programme/children-young-people/dance-in-schools/**

Left to their own devices, organisations sometimes struggle to find the right person, at a school, to talk to. So don't assume that there's nothing out there just because no one has contacted you. It's up to you to find what your young people need.

**The Centre for Advance Training in Dance** offers pre-vocational dance training, where a young person stays at their existing school, but goes for extra classes at the weekend. DFE funded. For young people showing excellent potential. Disabled and non-disabled. www.nationaldancecats.co.uk

**The National Youth Dance Company of England** takes on thirty young people a year, who can stay until they're 19. There are disabled young people in the company. Provides specialised tuition based around each person's needs.

Claire Somerville, One Dance UK

## Funding

Often, schools can't afford to employ extra staff themselves, or to get pupils to and from activities off-site. However, there are funding streams such as Awards for All. Schools can apply for grants of up to £10,000 through Awards for All to organise and extend extra-curricular provision. Set up in 1998 to allow non-profit making organisations to apply for lottery funding for specific projects, Awards for All aims to support community activity through its grants, which will:

- extend access and participation by encouraging more people to become actively involved in projects and activities;
- increase skill and creativity by supporting activities that help develop people and organisations, encourage talent and raise standards;
- improve quality of life by supporting local projects that improve people's opportunities, welfare, environment or facilities.

To apply, a school must first design a project with a community focus that corresponds to Awards for All's national and regional priorities.

These priorities can be ascertained by accessing Awards for All's website at www.biglotteryfund.org.uk/funding/funding-guidance/applying-for-funding. Assessors will look for evidence of real partnerships with outside organisations such as sports clubs, while wanting reassurance of the involvement of senior management in the application process, to ensure the school takes ownership of its project. In the past, some schools have merely been the passive recipients of services, paid for by grants, but without making the activity part of school life.

It is important to remember that Awards for All will not fund curriculum activity, as lottery money cannot be used for activities that are part of statutory obligations. This doesn't mean that equipment bought for the purposes of setting up a basketball club could not also be used during PE lessons. But an application to restock the school's PE cupboard will be rejected.

What Awards for All will fund, however, is transport to and from sporting and other activities. A major issue for many children with special educational needs who wish to access after-school clubs is their reliance on school transport to get them home. However, even though an Awards for All grant will help overcome this problem initially, innovative thinking is needed to sustain such a project long term.

*Figure 6.1* Sports wheelchairs are lighter, quicker and more manoeuvrable than other wheelchairs

Photo: David Evans, Fox Lane Photography.

## Case study – Sam, a pupil with spina bifida and hydrocephalus

Sam, an 11-year-old girl from Tamworth, has spina bifida and hydrocephalus. As she is a keen and budding athlete, Sam was provided with a sports wheelchair by Whizz-Kidz. One of a number of charities set up to assist children with physical disabilities and other special educational needs, Whizz-Kidz targets its support at youngsters under the age of 18, for whom the NHS is unable to provide much-needed mobility equipment, training and advice. (See the Whizz-Kidz website: www.whizz-kidz.org.uk)

Sam loved her wheelchair so much that when she recently grew out of it, she applied for a new one so that she could carry on enjoying sport with her friends. Her new wheelchair is light and manageable, was built specifically for her and is great for indoor and outdoor sports. She also uses it as her 'everyday' wheelchair so it meets all her needs – which is a good thing, as taking two wheelchairs in the car was a bit tricky for mum, with four kids!

Over the last five years, Sam has gained in confidence dramatically. She has used her sports wheelchair on her school sports day, and in wheelchair basketball games and weekly athletic sessions. Her latest hobby is non-contact boxing, which is good not only for her fitness and co-ordination but also a great way for her to make friends. Sam's sports wheelchair has given her a positive attitude towards her disability and having to use a wheelchair, and has also allowed her to enjoy many new hobbies.

Sam's mother says:

> The wheelchair has given Sam independence and a brighter outlook for the future. Without it she would have probably had to be pushed around in her wheelchairs for the rest of her life, never experiencing the freedom and independence that most of us take for granted.

Parents or carers of disabled children can contact the charity, which will then send out a trained therapist to assess the child's needs and lifestyle before considering the type of equipment best suited to them. Equipment is free (although those who can afford it may be asked to make a contribution towards costs) and can be designed to meet the specific needs of the young person.

Where there's a gap in a teacher's knowledge, SEND professionals can act as the expert, providing insights and advice about how best to do things. Professionals who are working in this field will already have a good idea of what works with a particular individual, and what doesn't.

> Talk to the SENDCO or Inclusion Manager – the person in charge of special needs provision in school. Find out what the young person's personal targets are and find a way that PE can help them achieve those targets. These might be as simple as listening for a few minutes, or tolerating water on their face.
>
> Anne Craddock, SEND PE consultant

In special schools, there are experienced professionals with many years' experience of adapting both curriculum content and delivery to meet a wide range of needs. Yet these are a very under-used resource in many areas. Partnerships between mainstream and special schools can be invaluable in facilitating a two-way exchange of knowledge, expertise and facilities.

> Young people in mainstream can join in a PE session at their local special school. Teachers can see what they're capable of, what sort of activities they can deliver.
>
> Neil Dawson, Head of PE, Wilson Stuart School

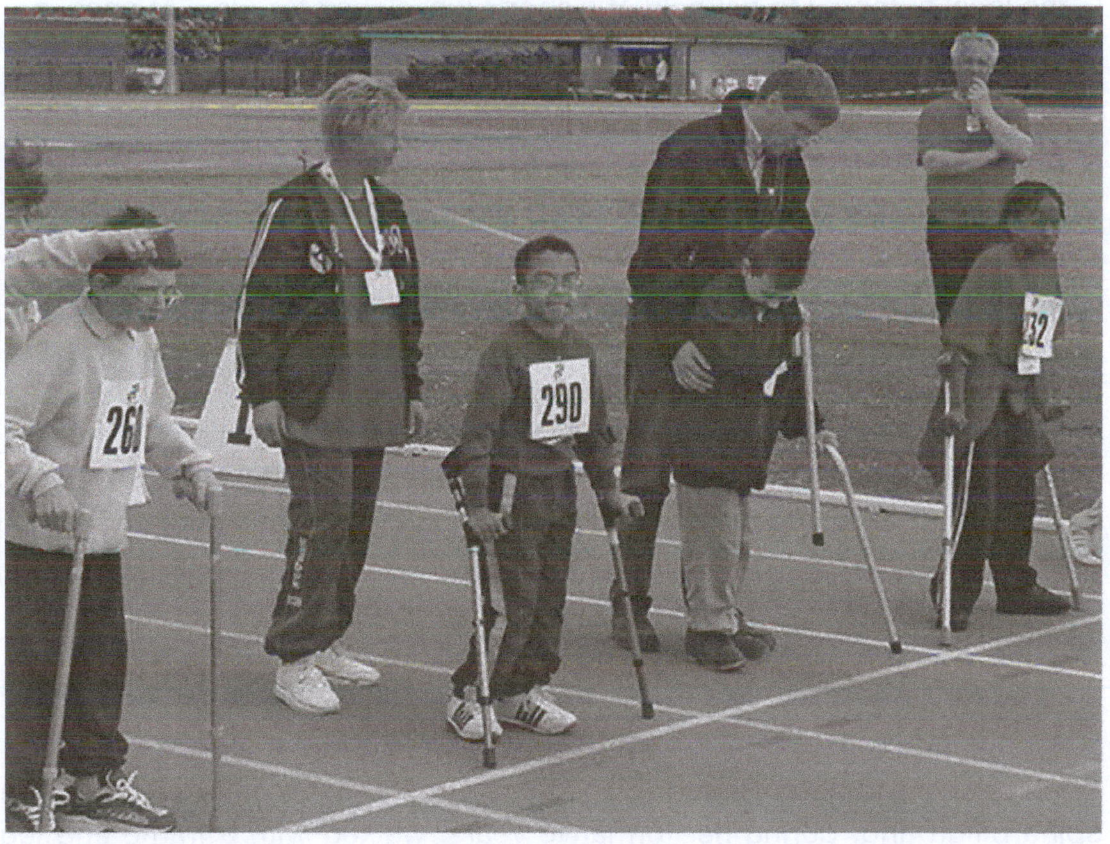


Photo: Simon Harris

Some special schools provide outreach services. The idea is to help teachers in mainstream schools become more aware of how to meet a wider range of specific needs and to expand those teachers' knowledge of the issues affecting children with SEND and their ability to access PE. These schools can also suggest practical solutions and offer advice on how to utilise and adapt teaching strategies. There might also be PE and sport sessions at the school that young people in mainstream can attend or that teachers in mainstream schools can observe.

## Case study – Alex, a pupil with cerebral palsy

Alex, a Year 7 child with cerebral palsy, was not accessing PE at his primary school. Walking with sticks, he couldn't do anything involving ball handling and often found himself on the sidelines during lessons. To him, PE was simply something other people did.

On arriving at secondary school, Alex once again found it difficult. He had extremely low confidence as regards his own capacity to take part and, initially, staff at the school found it difficult to adapt their activities so he could join in.

The turning point came when one of the teachers used his contacts with the local authority to get hold of a sports wheelchair for Alex. At once, a youngster who had struggled to move around during lessons was not only mobile, but could use his hands.

Suddenly, a whole host of possibilities were open to him. PE staff were now more confident in adapting activities. Playing basketball for the first time, a rule was introduced whereby every member of the team had to touch the ball prior to their team scoring a point. Focusing on 'man-to-man' marking in another lesson saw the shortest members of the class appointed to oppose Alex. Introducing these modifications from the start, rather than halfway through a lesson when it was realised that 'the kid in the wheelchair can't do it', prevented Alex from feeling he was being singled out. Similarly, other young people didn't think that their game was being changed for the worse, just because Alex couldn't do it.

## An inclusive experience

Britain's most famous Paralympian, Tanni Grey-Thompson, was born with spina bifida and, during her formative years, walked with a frame and leg braces. As she grew, her legs could no longer support her weight and, by the age of 7, she was in a wheelchair. Tanni says that she loved sport from an early age and was lucky at primary school because her friends and teachers supported her efforts.

'The children didn't look at me as different from them,' Tanni says. 'They didn't even think about discriminating against me. My best friend was always helping me up and down steps, and with my stuff. No one was horrible to me.'

She adds that the teachers always involved her in sport. 'When I hit the ball, because I couldn't move that quickly, the teacher said that the fielders could only walk to retrieve it, not run,' she says. 'I didn't even think about not being able to do PE. It was never an issue.'

When Tanni was 10, her parents sent her on a horse-riding holiday. 'Other mums with disabled kids who we knew were shocked. You're not letting Tanni go?' One mum said that her daughter couldn't go because she would miss her bedtime story and cuddles. The girl was 21. Tanni's parents didn't see her as being different just because she was in a wheelchair. They didn't wrap her in cotton wool. Tanni's mum just said, 'Are you going? Yes? Ok, you're off, bye.'

Tanni says:

> People thought my parents were hard on me, but I didn't see it that way. They were just keen to give me opportunities. Knew that I needed to be independent. There were no disabled toilets or drop curbs on that course at Bridgend. But I loved it. In a chair you were always the smallest. On a horse you were high up, bigger than everyone else.

At secondary school Tanni did tennis, swimming and athletics.

> Sometimes I had to be the time keeper, but mostly I was involved. We had a scary PE teacher called Ms Colville. In one of my first swimming lessons I was sat on the side-lines. She said 'Can you swim?' 'Yes.' 'Right: next week, you're swimming.' And that was it.

Sometimes Tanni had to go to the special school to do PE. They had specialist facilities and teachers, but she didn't like it there. 'All my friends were at my school. Playing sport with friends is important for girls. I did do my first wheelchair race at the special school, though.'

Tanni had supportive teachers and coaches who either modified her sporting activity accordingly or found sports that she could do, rather than fretting about involving her in sport because they feared she couldn't do certain things.

# Appendix 1 SEND legislation and guidance

## The Children and Families Act: a different landscape

The Children and Families Act 2014 introduced radical changes to the requirements placed on both schools and teachers regarding the education and inclusion of pupils with special educational needs and disabilities. The first major revision of the SEND framework for thirty years, it introduced a new system to help children with special educational needs and disabilities and shaped how education, health and social care professionals should work in partnership with children, young people and their families.

The reforms introduced a system to support children and young people from birth up to the age of 25, designed to ensure smooth transitions across all services as they move from school into further education, training and employment. The reforms give particular emphasis to preparing children and young people for adulthood from the earliest years. This means enabling children to be involved at as young an age as possible in all decisions relating to their learning, therapy, medical treatment and support from social care. The result of this preparation should be that when young people reach the age of 16, they are able to be full and active participants in all important decisions about their life.

There is now an important distinction made between a child and a young person. The Act gives significant new rights directly to young people when they are over compulsory school age but under the age of 25. Under the Act, a child becomes a young person after the last day of summer term during the academic year in which he or she turns 16. This is subject to a young person 'having capacity' to take a decision under the Mental Capacity Act 2005.

Throughout this book the term 'pupils with special educational needs and disabilities (SEND)' is used. A pupil has special educational needs if he or she:

- has a significantly greater difficulty in learning than the majority of others of the same age; or
- has a disability which prevents or hinders him or her from making use of facilities of a kind generally provided for others of the same age in mainstream schools or mainstream post-16 institutions.

(SEND Code of Practice 2015)

## *Section 19 principles*

Central to Part 3 of the Children and Families Act 2014 is Section 19. This section emphasises the role to be played by parents/carers and young people themselves in all decision-making about their SEND provision.

Part C of Section 19 issues a new challenge to schools in that there is a clear expectation not only that parents and pupils will be invited to participate but also that they should be supported to do so. This will certainly involve the provision of relevant information to parents but schools could also consider providing other forms of support: both practical support, such as helping with translation services, or even transport to attend important meetings, and emotional support, such as advocacy or pre-meetings to prepare parents and pupils to take a full part in all decisions. Many parents will need only a minimal level of additional support, but others – especially those often portrayed as 'hard to reach' – may require considerably more.

Key questions:

- Do you know the wishes and feelings about education of your pupils with SEND and their parents? If not, how can you find out?
- What could you and others in your subject/departmental team do to integrate this information into your planning for and delivery of teaching and learning?
- What more could you do to reach out to parents who may be anxious about or unwilling to engage with school?

## The SEND Code of Practice

As the quotation at the start of Chapter 1 makes clear, SEND provision is provision that is additional to or different from the high-quality, differentiated teaching to which all pupils are entitled. A school's first response to a pupil falling behind his or her peers should be to evaluate the quality of teaching and learning the pupil currently receives in all subjects. The pupil should be identified as having SEND only when the school is confident that all teaching is differentiated appropriately to meet that individual pupil's needs.

Once a pupil is identified as having SEND, schools are required to do whatever they can to remove any barriers to learning and to put in place effective provision, or 'SEND support'. This support must enable pupils with SEND to achieve the best possible outcomes.

Most schools and academies welcome pupils with a range of vulnerabilities, including special educational needs and disabilities, but may hesitate about including those with significant or complex needs. The reasons behind this reluctance are often a lack of expertise in an area of need, worries about behaviour and, most commonly expressed, concerns about the impact of that pupil's needs on the education of others.

The SEND Code of Practice is very clear that where the parent of a pupil with an Education, Health and Care plan (EHC plan) makes a request for a particular school, the local authority *must* comply with that preference and name the school in the plan unless:

- it would be unsuitable for the age, ability, aptitude or SEN of the child or young person, or
- the attendance of the child or young person there would be incompatible with the efficient education of others, or the efficient use of resources.

(DfE 2015, 9.79, p. 172)

Legally, schools cannot refuse to admit a pupil who does not have an EHC plan because they do not feel able to cater for his or her needs, or because the pupil does not have an EHC plan.

## *Outcomes*

Outcomes are written from the perspective of the pupil and should identify what the provision is intended to achieve. For example, do you think the following is an outcome for a pupil in Year 7 with literacy difficulties?

> For the next 10 weeks Jake will work on an online literacy program for 20 minutes three times each week.

It may be specific and measurable; it is achievable and realistic; and it is time targeted, so it is 'SMART' but it isn't an 'outcome'. What is described here is provision, i.e. the intervention that the school will use to help Jake to make accelerated progress.

Outcomes are intended to look forward to the end of the next stage or phase of education, usually two or three years hence. Teachers will, of course, set short-term targets covering between six and twelve weeks, and education and health plans will also include interim objectives to be discussed at annual reviews. So, what would be an outcome for Jake?

> By the end of Year 9, Jake will be able to read and understand the textbooks for his chosen GCSE courses.

The online literacy course would then form a part of the package of provision to enable Jake to achieve this outcome.

## The graduated approach

The SEND Code of Practice describes SEND support as a cyclical process of assess, plan, do and review that is known as the 'graduated approach'. This cycle is already commonly used in schools, and for pupils with SEND it is intended to be much more than a token, in-house process. Rather it should be a powerful mechanism for reflection and evaluation of the impact of SEND provision. Through the four-part cycle, decisions and actions are revisited, refined and revised. This then leads to a deeper understanding of an individual pupil's needs whilst also offering an insight into the effectiveness of the school's overall provision for pupils with SEND. The graduated approach offers the school, the pupil and his or her parents a growing understanding of needs and of what provision the pupil requires to enable him or her to make good progress and secure good outcomes. Through successive cycles, the graduated approach draws on increasingly specialist expertise, assessments and approaches, and more frequent reviews. This structured process gives teachers the information they need to match specific, evidence-based interventions to pupils' individual needs.

### *Evidence-based interventions*

In recent years, a number of universities and other research organisations have produced evidence about the efficacy of a range of different interventions for vulnerable pupils and pupils with SEND. Most notable among this research is that sponsored by the Education Endowment Fund that offers schools valid data on the impact of interventions and the optimal conditions for their use. Other important sources of information about evidence-based interventions for specific areas of need are the Communication Trust 'What Works?' website and 'Interventions for Literacy' from the SpLD/Dyslexia Trust. Both sites offer transparent and clear information for professionals and parents to support joint decisions about provision.

## The Equality Act 2010

Sitting alongside the Children and Families Act 2014, the requirements of the Equality Act 2010 remain firmly in place. This is especially important because many children and young people who have SEND may also have a disability under the Equality Act. The definition of disability in the Equality Act is that the child or young person has 'a physical or mental impairment which has a long-term and substantial adverse effect on a person's ability to carry out normal day-to-day activities'.

'Long-term' is defined as lasting or being likely to last for 'a year or more', and 'substantial' is defined as 'more than minor or trivial'. The definition includes sensory impairments such as those affecting sight or hearing, and, just as crucially for schools, children with long-term health conditions such as asthma, diabetes, epilepsy and cancer.

As the SEND Code of Practice (DfE 2015, p. 16) states, the definition for disability provides a relatively low threshold, and includes many more children than schools may realise. Children and young people with some conditions do not necessarily have SEND, but there is often a significant overlap between disabled children and young people and those with SEND. Where a disabled child or young person requires special educational provision, they will also be covered by the SEND duties.

The Equality Act applies to all schools including academies and free schools, university technical colleges and studio schools, and also further education colleges and sixth form colleges – even where the school or college has no disabled pupils currently on roll. This is because the duties under the Equality Act are anticipatory in that they cover not only current pupils but also prospective ones. The expectation is that all schools will be reviewing accessibility continually and making reasonable adjustments in order to improve access for disabled pupils. When thinking about disabled access, the first thing that school leaders usually consider is physical access, such as wheelchair access, lifts and ramps. But physical access is only part of the requirement of the Equality Act and often is the simplest to improve. Your school's accessibility plan for disabled pupils must address all of three elements of planned improvements in access:

1. physical improvements to increase access to education and associated services;
2. improvements in access to the curriculum;
3. improvements in the provision of information for disabled pupils in a range of formats.

Improvements in access to the curriculum are often a harder nut to crack as they involve all departments and all teachers looking closely at their teaching and learning strategies and evaluating how effectively these meet the needs of disabled pupils. Often, relatively minor amendments to the curriculum or teaching approaches can lead to major improvements in access for disabled pupils, and these often have a positive impact on the education of all pupils. For example, one school installed a Soundfield amplification system in a number of classrooms because a pupil with a hearing loss had joined the school. The following year, the cohort of Year 7 pupils had particularly poor speaking and listening skills and it was noticed that they were more engaged in learning when they were taught in the rooms with the Soundfield system. This led to improvements in progress for the whole cohort and significantly reduced the level of disruption and off-task behaviours in those classes.

Schools also have wider duties under the Equality Act to prevent discrimination, to promote equality of opportunity, and to foster good relations. These duties should inform all aspects of school improvement planning from curriculum design through to anti-bullying policies and practice.

Significantly, a pupil's underachievement or behaviour difficulties might relate to an underlying physical or mental impairment which could be covered by the Equality Act. Each pupil is different and will respond to situations in his or her unique way so a disability should be considered in the context of the child as an individual. The 'social model' of disability sees the environment as the primary disabling factor, as opposed to the 'medical model' that focuses on the individual child's needs and difficulties. School activities and environments should be considered in the light of possible barriers to learning or participation.

# Appendix 2 Departmental policy

Whether the practice in your school is to have separate SEND policies for each department or to embed the information on SEND in your whole-school inclusion or teaching and learning policies, the processes and information detailed below will still be relevant.

Good practice for pupils with SEND and disabilities is good practice for all pupils, especially those who are 'vulnerable' to underachievement. Vulnerable groups may include looked-after children (LAC), pupils for whom English is an additional language (EAL), pupils from minority ethnic groups, young carers, and pupils known to be eligible for free school meals/Pupil Premium funding. Be especially aware of those pupils with SEND who face one or more additional vulnerabilities and for whom effective support might need to go beyond help in the classroom.

It is crucial that your departmental or faculty policy describes a strategy for meeting pupils' special educational needs within your particular curricular area. The policy should set the scene for any visitor, from supply staff to inspectors, and make a valuable contribution to the department handbook. The process of developing a departmental SEND policy offers the opportunity to clarify and evaluate current thinking and practice within the PE team and to establish a consistent approach.

The SEND policy for your department is a significant document in terms of the leadership and management of your subject. The preparation and review of the policy should be led by a senior manager within the team because that person needs to have sufficient status to be able to influence subsequent practice and training across the department.

## What should a departmental policy contain?

The starting points for your departmental SEND policy will be the whole-school SEND policy and the SEND Information Report that, under the Children and

Families Act 2014, all schools are required to publish. Each subject department's own policy should then 'flesh out' the detail in a way that describes how things will work in practice. Writing the policy needs to be much more than a paper exercise completed merely to satisfy the senior management team and Ofsted inspectors. Rather, it is an opportunity for your staff to come together as a team to create a framework for teaching PE in a way that makes your subject accessible, not only to pupils with special educational needs and disabilities but to all pupils in the school. It is also an ideal opportunity to discuss the impact of grouping on academic and social outcomes for pupils. (Bear in mind that the Code of Practice includes a specific duty that 'schools must ensure that pupils with SEND engage in the activities of the school alongside pupils who do not have SEND' (6.2, p. 92).

We need to be careful in PE that, when grouping pupils, we take into account a range of factors. It is vital that social issues are also considered if pupils are to be able to learn effectively. Having a complement of pupils with good ability and well-developed social skills will lift the attitude and attainment of everybody within a group.

## Who should be involved in developing your SEND policy?

The job of developing and reviewing your policy will be easier if tackled as a joint endeavour. Involve people who will be able to offer support and guidance such as:

- the school SEND governor;
- the SENCO or other school leader with responsibility for SEND;
- your support staff, including teaching assistants and technicians;
- the school data manager, who will be able to offer information about the attainment and progress of different groups;
- outside experts from your sports organisations, your academy chain or other schools;
- parents of pupils with SEND;
- pupils themselves – both with and without SEND.

Bringing together a range of views and information will enable you to develop a policy that is compliant with the letter *and* principle of the legislation, that is relevant to the context of your school, and that is useful in guiding practice and improving outcomes for all pupils.

### *The role of parents in developing your departmental SEND policy*

As outlined in Appendix 1, Section 19 of the Children and Families Act 2014 raises the bar of expectations about how parents should be involved in and influence the work of schools. Not only is it best practice to involve parents of pupils with SEND in the development of policy, but it will also help in 'getting it right' for both pupils and staff. There are a number of ways, both formal and informal, to find out the views of parents to inform policy writing, including:

- a focus group;
- a coffee morning/drop-in;
- a questionnaire/online survey;
- a phone survey of a sample of parents.

Parents will often respond more readily if the request for feedback or the invitation to attend a meeting comes from their son or daughter.

## Where to start when writing a policy

An audit can act as a starting point for reviewing current policy on SEND or writing a new policy. This will involve gathering information and reviewing current practice with regard to pupils with SEND, and is best completed by the whole department, preferably with some input from the SENCO or another member of staff with responsibility for SEND within the school. An audit carried out by the whole department provides a valuable opportunity for professional development so long as it is seen as an exercise in sharing good practice and encourages joint planning. It may also facilitate your department's contribution to the school provision map. But, before embarking on an audit, it is worth investing some time in a departmental meeting, or ideally a training day, to raise awareness of the legislation around special educational needs and disabilities and to establish a shared philosophy across your department.

The following headings may be useful when you are establishing your departmental policy:

### *General statement of compliance*

- What is the overarching aim of the policy? What outcomes do you want to achieve for pupils with SEND?
- How are you complying with legislation and guidance?
- What does the school SEND Information Report say about teaching and learning and provision for pupils with SEND?

**Example**

All members of the department will ensure that the needs of all pupils with SEND are met, according to the aims of the school and its SEND policy . . .

## *Definition of SEND*

- What does SEND mean?
- What are the areas of need and the categories used in the Code of Practice?
- Are there any special implications for your subject area?

(See Chapter 1.)

## *Provision for staff within the department*

- Who has responsibility for SEND within the department?
- What are the responsibilities of this role? E.g.

  - liaison between the department and the SENCO;
  - monitoring the progress of and outcomes for pupils with SEND, e.g. identifying attainment gaps between pupils with SEND and their peers;
  - attending any liaison meetings and providing feedback to colleagues;
  - attending and contributing to training;
  - maintaining departmental SEND information and records;
  - representing the needs of pupils with SEND at departmental level;
  - liaising with parents of pupils with SEND;
  - gathering feedback from pupils with SEND on the impact of teaching and support strategies on their learning and wellbeing;

- (The post can be seen as a valuable development opportunity for staff, and the name of this person should be included in the policy. However, where responsibility for SEND is given to a relatively junior member of the team, there must be support and supervision from the head of the department to ensure that the needs of pupils with SEND have sufficient prominence in both policy and practice.)
- What information about pupils' SEND is held, where is it stored and how is it shared?
- How can staff access additional resources, information and training?
- How will staff ensure effective planning and communication between teachers and teaching assistants?
- What assessments are available for teachers in your department to support accurate identification of SEND?

**Example**

The member of staff with responsibility for overseeing the provision of SEND within the department will attend liaison meetings and subsequently give feedback to the other members of the department. S/he will maintain the department's SEND file, attend and/or organise appropriate training and disseminate this to all departmental staff. All information will be treated with confidentiality.

### *Provision for pupils with SEND*

- How are pupils' special educational needs identified? E.g.
    - observation in lessons;
    - assessment of class work/homework;
    - end of module tests/progress checks;
    - annual examinations/SATs/GCSEs;
    - reports;
- How is progress measured for pupils with SEND?
- How do members of the department contribute to individual learning plans, meetings with parents and reviews?
- What criteria are used for organising teaching groups?
- How/when can pupils move between groups?
- What adjustments are made for pupils with special educational needs and/or disabilities in lessons and homework?
- How do we use information about pupils' abilities in reading, writing, speaking and listening when planning lessons and homework?
- What alternative courses are available for pupils with SEND?
- What special arrangements are made for internal and external examinations?
- What guidance is available for working effectively with support staff?

Here is a good place also to put a statement about the school behaviour policy and any rewards and sanctions, and how the department will make any necessary adjustments to meet the needs of pupils with SEND.

**Example**

The staff in the PE department will aim to support pupils with SEND to achieve the best possible outcomes. They will do this by supporting pupils to achieve their individual targets as specified in their individual learning plans, and will provide feedback for progress reviews. Pupils with SEND will be included in the departmental monitoring system used for all pupils.

### *Resources and learning materials*

- Is any specialist equipment used in the department?
- How are differentiated resources developed? What criteria do we use (e.g. literacy levels)?
- Where are resources stored and are they accessible for both staff and pupils?

**Example**

The department will provide suitably differentiated materials and, where appropriate, specialist resources to meet the needs of pupils with SEND. Alternative courses and examinations will be made available where appropriate for individual pupils. Support staff will be provided with curriculum information in advance of lessons and will be involved in lesson planning. A list of resources is available in the department handbook.

### *Staff qualifications and continuing professional development (CPD)*

- What qualifications and experience do the members of the department have?
- What training has already taken place, and when? What impact did that training have on teaching and learning, and progress for pupils with SEND?
- How is training planned? What criteria are used to identify training needs?
- What account of SEND is taken when new training opportunities are proposed?
- Is a record kept of training completed and ongoing training needs?

**Example**

A record of training undertaken, specialist skills and training required will be kept in the department handbook. Requests for training will be considered in line with the department and school improvement plan.

### *Monitoring and reviewing the policy*

- How will the policy be monitored?
- Who will lead the monitoring?
- When will the policy be reviewed?

**Example**

The departmental SEND policy will be monitored by the head of department on a planned annual basis, with advice being sought from the SENCO as part of the three-yearly review process.

## Conclusion

Creating a departmental SEND policy should be a developmental activity that will improve teaching and learning for all pupils, but especially for those who are vulnerable to underachievement. The policy should be a working document that will evolve and change over time; it is there to challenge current practice and to encourage improvement for both pupils and staff. If departmental staff work together to create the policy, they will have ownership of it; it will have true meaning and be effective in clarifying good practice.

An example of a departmental *policy* for you to amend is available on the website: www.routledge.com/9781138209015.

# Appendix 3 Different types of SEND

## Introduction

This appendix is a starting point for information on the special educational needs most frequently encountered in mainstream schools. It describes the main characteristics of each area of special educational need and disability (SEND) with practical ideas for use in subject areas, and contacts for further information.

There is a measure of repetition, as some strategies prove to be effective with a whole range of pupils (and often with those who have no identified SEND). However, the layout enables readers an 'at a glance' reminder of effective approaches and facilitates copying for colleagues and TAs.

The SEND Code of Practice (DfE 2015) outlines four broad areas of need. These are:

- communication and interaction;
- cognition and learning;
- social, emotional and mental health difficulties;
- sensory and/or physical needs.

These broad areas are not exclusive and pupils may have needs that cut across some or all of them. Equally, pupils' difficulties and needs will change over time. The terms used in this chapter are helpful when reviewing and monitoring special educational provision, but pupils' individual talents and interests are just as important as their disability or special educational need. Because of this, specific terms or labels need to be used with care in discussion with parents, pupils or other professionals. Unless a pupil has a firm diagnosis, and parents and pupil understand the implications of that diagnosis, it is more appropriate to describe the features of the special educational need rather than use the label. For example, a teacher might describe a pupil's co-ordination difficulties but not use the term 'dyspraxia'.

There is a continuum of need within each of the special educational needs and disabilities listed here. Some pupils will be affected more than others and show fewer or more of the characteristics described.

Pupils with other, less common special educational needs may be included in some schools, and additional information on these conditions may be found in a variety of sources. These include the school SENCO, local authority support services, educational psychologists and online information, for example on the Nasen SEND Gateway and disability charity websites such as those of Mencap, CAF or I CAN, the children's communication charity.

**Further information**

www.nasen.org.uk
www.mencap.org.uk
www.cafamily.org.uk
www.ican.org.uk

## Asperger syndrome

Asperger (or Asperger's) syndrome is a type of autism. People with Asperger syndrome do not have 'learning difficulties' as such, but they do have difficulties associated with being on the austistic spectrum. They often want to make friends but do not understand the complex rules of social interaction. They may have impaired fine and gross motor skills, with writing being a particular problem. Boys are more likely to be affected – with the ratio being 10:1 boys to girls. Because they appear 'odd' and naive, these pupils are particularly vulnerable to bullying.

### *Main characteristics*

- **Social interaction**
  Pupils with Asperger syndrome want friends but have not developed the strategies necessary for making and sustaining friendships. They find it very difficult to learn social norms and to pick up on social cues. Highly social situations, such as lessons, can cause great anxiety.

- **Social communication**
  Pupils have appropriate spoken language but tend to sound formal and pedantic, using little expression and an unusual tone of voice. They have difficulty using and understanding non-verbal language, such as facial expression, gesture, body language and eye contact. They have a literal understanding of language and do not grasp implied meanings.

- **Social imagination**
  Pupils with Asperger syndrome need structured environments and routines they understand and can anticipate. They may excel at learning facts and figures but have difficulty understanding abstract concepts and in generalising information and skills. They often have all-consuming special interests.

### *How can the PE teacher help?*

- Liaise closely with parents, especially over homework.
- Create as calm an environment as possible.
- Allow the pupil to work in the same place/position where possible.
- Set up a buddy system.
- Provide additional visual cues.
- Give time for the pupil to process questions and respond.
- Make sure pupils understand what to do.
- Allow alternatives to writing for recording.
- Use visual timetables and task activity lists.

- Prepare for changes to routines well in advance.
- Give written homework instructions and stick them into an exercise book.
- Have your own rules and apply them consistently.

**Further information**

www.autism.org.uk/about/what-is/asperger.aspx

## Attention deficit disorder (with or without hyperactivity) ADD/ADHD

Attention deficit hyperactivity disorder is one of the most common childhood disorders and can continue through adolescence and adulthood. ADHD can occur in pupils of any intellectual ability and may also cause additional problems, such as sleep and anxiety disorders. The features of ADHD usually diminish with age, but many individuals who are diagnosed with the condition at a young age will continue to experience problems in adulthood.

### *Main characteristics*

- short attention span or easily distracted by noise and movement
- difficulty in following instructions and completing tasks
- difficulty in listening to and processing verbal instructions
- restlessness, inability to keep still causing frequent fidgeting
- difficulty with moderating behaviour such as constant talking, interrupting and calling out
- difficulty in waiting or taking turns
- impulsivity – acting without thinking about consequences

### *How can the PE teacher help?*

- Make eye contact and use the pupil's name when speaking to him.
- Keep instructions simple – the one sentence rule.
- Provide clear routines and rules, rehearse them regularly.
- Sit the pupil away from obvious distractions, e.g. windows, the computer.
- In busy situations direct the pupil by name to visual or practical objects.
- Encourage the pupil to repeat back instructions before starting work.
- Tell the pupil when to begin a task.
- Give two choices – avoid the option of the pupil saying 'No', e.g. 'Do you want to use your left or right foot to pass the ball?'
- Give advanced warning when something is about to happen. Change or finish with a time, e.g. 'In two minutes I need you (pupil name) to . . .'
- Give specific praise – catch the pupil being good, give attention for positive behaviour.
- Give the pupil responsibilities so that others can see him in a positive light and he develops a positive self-image.
- Know what a particular child's triggers are. For some it could be sugar, whereas for others sugar has a calming effect. So watch out for the drinks they bring with them to PE lessons and sport sessions. Others could find being in a noisy, packed sports hall difficult.

**Further information**

| | | |
|---|---|---|
| ADDISS | 020 8952 2800 | www.addiss.co.uk |
| ADHD Foundation | 0151 237 2661 | www.adhdfoundation.org.uk |
| Young Minds | 020 7089 5050 | www.youngminds.org.uk |
| Autism (ASD) | | |

## Autistic spectrum disorders (ASD)

The term 'autistic spectrum disorders' is used for a range of disorders affecting the development of social interaction, social communication and social imagination and flexibility of thought. This is known as the 'Triad of Impairments'. Pupils with ASD cover the full range of ability, and the severity of the impairment varies widely. Some pupils also have learning disabilities or other difficulties. Four times as many boys as girls are diagnosed with an ASD.

### *Main characteristics*

- **Social interaction**
  Pupils with an ASD find it difficult to understand social behaviour and this affects their ability to interact with children and adults. They do not always understand social contexts. They may experience high levels of stress and anxiety in settings that do not meet their needs or when routines are changed. This can lead to inappropriate behaviour.

- **Social communication**
  Understanding and use of non-verbal and verbal communication are impaired. Pupils with an ASD have difficulty understanding the communication of others and in developing effective communication themselves. They have a literal understanding of language. Many are delayed in learning to speak, and some never develop speech at all.

- **Social imagination and flexibility of thought**
  Pupils with an ASD have difficulty in thinking and behaving flexibly which may result in restricted, obsessional, or repetitive activities. They are often more interested in objects than people, and have intense interests in one particular area such as trains or vacuum cleaners. Pupils work best when they have a routine. Unexpected changes in those routines will cause distress. Some pupils with autistic spectrum disorders have a different perception of sounds, sights, smell, touch and taste, and this can affect their response to these sensations.

### *How can the PE teacher help?*

- Liaise with parents as they will have many useful strategies.
- Provide visual supports in class: objects, pictures, etc.
- Establish a visual timetable of the lesson, so children know what is happening and what will come next. Showing them a towel acts as a sign that it is time to get out of the pool, whereas a ball might mean that it is time to begin the activity.
- Give a symbolic or written timetable for each day.

- Give advance warning of any changes to usual routines.
- Provide either an individual learning area or a work buddy.
- Avoid using too much eye contact as it can cause distress.
- Give individual instructions linked to visual demonstration, using the pupil's name, e.g. 'Paul, stand on the line like John is doing.'
- Allow access to computers.
- Develop social interactions using a buddy system or Circle of Friends.
- Avoid using metaphor, idiom or sarcasm – say what you mean in simple language.
- Use special interests to motivate.
- Allow difficult situations to be rehearsed by means of Social Stories.

**Further information**

| | | |
|---|---|---|
| The National Autistic Society | 020 7833 2299 | www.autism.org.uk |
| Autism Education Trust | 0207 903 3650 | www.autismeducationtrust.org.uk |

## Cerebral palsy (CP)

Cerebral palsy is a condition that affects muscle control and movement. It is usually caused by an injury to the brain before, during or after birth. Pupils with cerebral palsy have difficulties in controlling their muscles and movements as they grow and develop. Problems vary from slight clumsiness to more severe lack of control of movements. Pupils with CP may also have learning difficulties. They may use a wheelchair or other mobility aid.

### *Main characteristics*

There are three main forms of cerebral palsy:

- **spastic cerebral palsy** – associated with stiff or tight muscle tone, resulting in a decreased range of movement; this stiffening of muscle tone can be very painful and affect different parts of the body
- **dyskenetic cerebral palsy** – sustained or intermittent involuntary muscle contractions often affecting the whole body
- **ataxic cerebral palsy** – an inability to activate the correct pattern of muscles during movement, resulting in an unsteady gait with balance difficulties and poor spatial awareness

Pupils with CP may also have communication difficulties.

### *How can the PE teacher help?*

- Talk to parents, the physiotherapist – and the pupil.
- Physiotherapy targets are usually based around developing strength, stamina and flexibility and can be used as part of whole-class warm-ups.
- Consider the layout of the learning environment.
- Have high academic expectations.
- Use visual supports: objects, pictures, symbols.
- Arrange for a work or subject buddy.
- Speak directly to the pupil rather than through a teaching assistant.
- Ensure access to appropriate equipment.

**Further information**

Scope 0808 800 3333 www.scope.org.uk

## Down's syndrome (DS)

Down's syndrome is the most common identifiable cause of learning disability. This is a genetic condition caused by the presence of an extra chromosome 21. People with DS have varying degrees of learning difficulties ranging from mild to severe. They have a specific learning profile with characteristic strengths and weaknesses. All share certain physical characteristics but will also inherit family traits, in physical features and personality. They may have additional sight, hearing, respiratory and heart problems.

### *Main characteristics*

- delayed motor skills
- takes longer to learn and consolidate new skills
- limited concentration
- difficulties with generalisation, thinking and reasoning
- sequencing difficulties
- stronger visual than aural skills
- better social than academic skills

### *How can the PE teacher help?*

- Ensure that the pupil is in the best position to see and hear.
- Speak directly to the pupil and reinforce with facial expression, pictures and objects.
- Use simple, familiar language in short sentences – stressing one aspect at a time. Abstract instructions such as 'Get in a good defensive position and remember to mark number 5' are likely to result in confusion. Use direct language: 'Keep close to number 5. Stop number 5 from getting the ball. If number 5 gets the ball, try to tackle him and take the ball from him.'
- Check instructions have been understood.
- Give time for the pupil to process information and formulate a response.
- Break lessons up into a series of shorter, varied and achievable tasks.
- Accept other ways of recording: drawings, tape/video recordings, symbols, etc.
- Set differentiated tasks linked to the work of the rest of the class.
- Provide age-appropriate resources and activities.
- Allow working in top sets to give good behaviour models.
- Provide a work buddy.
- Expect unsupported work for part of each lesson.

**Further information**

| | | |
|---|---|---|
| Down's Syndrome Association | 020 8682400 | www.downs-syndrome.org.uk |

## Foetal alcohol syndrome

Foetal alcohol syndrome (FAS) or foetal alcohol spectrum disorders (FASD) are umbrella terms for diagnoses relating to a child's exposure to alcohol before birth. Alcohol can affect the development of all cells and organs, but it is the brain and nervous system that are particularly vulnerable. Each person with FAS/D may face a range of difficulties across a spectrum from mild to severe.

### *Main characteristics:*

- visual impairment
- sleep problems
- speech and language delay
- impulsivity and/or hyperactivity
- memory problems
- inappropriate social behaviour

### *How can the PE teacher help?*

- Gather information from parents and other professionals involved with the pupil to find the most effective ways of teaching him/her (perhaps through the SENCO in the first instance).
- Find out the pupil's strengths and use these as starting points for learning.
- Keep instructions simple and offer information in verbal and visual form.
- Ensure routines are explicit and followed consistently.
- Use concrete and positive language, e.g. 'Walk' rather than 'Don't run'.
- Check the pupil knows and understands any school or class rules and rules for team games.
- Specify clearly what is expected for any task or activity.
- Provide a memory mat or audio recording facilities to support retention of information.

**Further information**

www.drinkaware.co.uk/fas

## Fragile X syndrome

Fragile X syndrome is caused by a malformation of the X chromosome and is the most common form of inherited learning disability. This intellectual disability varies widely, with up to a third having learning problems ranging from moderate to severe. More boys than girls are affected, but both may be carriers.

### *Main characteristics*

- delayed and disordered speech and language development
- difficulties with the social use of language
- articulation and/or fluency difficulties
- verbal skills better developed than reasoning skills
- repetitive or obsessive behaviour, such as hand-flapping, chewing, etc.
- clumsiness and fine motor co-ordination problems
- attention deficit and hyperactivity
- easily anxious or overwhelmed in busy environments

### *How can the PE teacher help?*

- Liaise with parents.
- Make sure the pupil knows what is to happen in each lesson – provide visual timetables, work schedules or written lists.
- Ensure the pupil sits at the front of the class, in the same seat for all lessons.
- Arrange a work/subject buddy.
- Where possible, keep to routines and give prior warning of all changes.
- Make instructions clear and simple.
- Use visual supports: objects, pictures, symbols.
- Allow the pupil to use a computer to record and access information.
- Give lots of praise and positive feedback.

### Further information

Fragile X Society, Rood End House, 6 Stortford Road, Dunmow, CM6 1DA
01424 813147 (Helpline); 01371 875100 (Office)
www.fragilex.org.uk

## Learning disability (learning difficulty)

The terms 'learning disability' and 'learning difficulty' are used to describe a wide continuum of difficulties ranging from moderate (MLD) to profound and multiple (PMLD). Pupils with learning disabilities find it harder to understand, learn and remember new things, meaning they may have problems across a range of areas such as communication, being aware of risks or managing everyday tasks.

### *Moderate learning difficulties (MLD)*

The term 'moderate learning difficulties' is used to describe pupils who find it extremely difficult to achieve expected levels of attainment across the curriculum, even with a well-differentiated and flexible approach to teaching. These pupils do not find learning easy and can suffer from low self-esteem and sometimes exhibit unacceptable behaviour as a way of avoiding failure. For all pupils with learning disabilities, the social aspect of school is a crucial element in their development and understanding of the 'culture' of young people, so it is important for them to have friends who don't have learning disabilities as well as those who do. As the SEND Code of Practice says at 6.2 (p. 92): 'Schools must . . . ensure that children and young people with SEN engage in the activities of the school alongside pupils who do not have SEN.'

#### *Main characteristics*

- difficulties with reading, writing and comprehension
- difficulties in understanding and retaining basic mathematical skills and concepts
- immature social and emotional skills
- limited vocabulary and communication skills
- short attention span
- under-developed co-ordination skills
- lack of logical reasoning
- inability to transfer and apply skills to different situations
- difficulty remembering what has been taught
- difficulty with organising themselves, following a timetable, remembering books and equipment

#### *How can the PE teacher help?*

- Check the pupil's strengths, weaknesses and attainment levels.
- Establish a routine within the lesson.
- Allow for repetition of content but provide a variety of short approaches to this content.

- Keep listening tasks short or broken up with activities.
- Provide word lists, writing frames, shortened text.
- Try alternative methods of recording information, e.g. drawings, charts, labelling, diagrams, use of ICT.
- Check previously gained knowledge and build on this.
- Repeat information in different ways.
- Show the child what to do or what the expected outcome is; demonstrate or show examples of completed work.
- Use practical, concrete, visual examples to illustrate explanations.
- Question the pupil to check they have grasped a concept or can follow instructions.
- Make sure the pupil always has something to do.
- Use lots of praise, instant rewards – catch them trying hard.

## *Severe learning difficulties (SLD)*

This term covers a wide and varied group of pupils who have significant intellectual or cognitive impairments. Many have communication difficulties and/or sensory impairments in addition to more general cognitive impairments. They may also have difficulties in mobility, co-ordination and perception. Some pupils may use signs and symbols to support their communication and understanding. Pupils' academic attainment will vary, with some being able to access a well-differentiated mainstream curriculum and achieve at GCSE level; others may achieve within the upper P scale range (P4–P8) for much of their school careers.

### *How can the PE teacher help?*

- Liaise with parents.
- Arrange a work/subject buddy.
- Use visual supports: objects, pictures, symbols.
- Learn some signs relevant to the subject.
- Allow the pupil time to process information and formulate responses.
- Set differentiated tasks linked to the work of the rest of the class.
- Set achievable targets for each lesson or module of work.
- Accept different recording methods: drawings, audio or video recordings, photographs, etc.
- Give access to computers where appropriate.
- Give a series of short, varied activities within each lesson. Chaining skills – breaking them down into parts, building up to the whole is a useful technique. So, to throw a ball: look at the target – practise – keep your head still – practise – stand with feet shoulder width apart to keep balance – practise – non-throwing foot forward – practise.

## *Profound and multiple learning difficulties (PMLD)*

Pupils with profound and multiple learning difficulties have complex learning needs. In addition to very severe learning difficulties, pupils have other significant difficulties, such as physical disabilities, sensory impairments or severe medical conditions. Pupils with PMLD require a high level of adult support, both for their learning needs and for their personal care.

They are able to access the curriculum through sensory experiences and stimulation. Some pupils communicate by gesture, eye pointing or symbols, others by very simple language.

### *How can the PE teacher help?*

- Liaise with parents and teaching assistants.
- Identify possible sensory experiences in your lessons.
- Use additional sensory supports: objects, pictures, fragrances, music, movements, food, etc.
- Take photographs to record experiences and responses.
- Set up a buddy rota for the class.
- Identify times when the pupil can work with groups, as using physical activity to engage a child in social interaction can help them immensely.
- Provide choices and experiences alongside non-disabled peers. Children may not be able to jump up and down, but they can move certain parts of their body in the same way.

**Further information**

| | | |
|---|---|---|
| Mencap | 020 7454 0454 | www.mencap.org.uk |
| Foundation for People with Learning Disabilities | 020 7803 1100 | www.learningdisabilities.org.uk |

## Physical disability (PD)

There is a wide range of physical disabilities, and pupils with PD cover all academic abilities. Some pupils are able to access the curriculum and learn effectively without additional educational provision. They have a disability but do not have a special educational need. For other pupils the impact on their education may be severe, and the school will need to make adjustments to enable them to access the curriculum.

Some pupils with a physical disability have associated medical conditions which may impact on their mobility. These include cerebral palsy, heart disease, spina bifida and hydrocephalus, and muscular dystrophy. Pupils with physical disabilities may also have sensory impairments, neurological problems or learning difficulties. They may use a wheelchair and/or additional mobility aids. Some pupils will be mobile but may have significant fine motor difficulties that require support. Others may need augmentative or alternative communication aids.

Pupils with a physical disability may need to miss lessons to attend physiotherapy or medical appointments. They are also likely to become very tired as they expend greater effort to complete everyday tasks. Schools will need to be flexible and sensitive to individual pupil needs.

### *How can the PE teacher help?*

- Get to know pupils and parents, and they will help you make the right adjustments.
- Maintain high expectations.
- Consider the changing room layout.
- Allow extra time for getting changed.
- Allow the pupil to leave lessons a few minutes early to avoid busy corridors and give time to get to the next lesson.
- Speak directly to the pupil rather than through a teaching assistant.
- Let pupils make their own decisions.
- Ensure access to appropriate equipment for the lesson.
- Give alternative ways of participating.
- Be sensitive to fatigue, especially at the end of the school day.

**Further information**

Scope 0808 800 3333 www.scope.org.uk

## Social, emotional and mental health difficulties

This area includes pupils who experience a wide range of difficulties characterised in a number of ways, including becoming withdrawn or exhibiting behavioural difficulties. Behaviours such as these may reflect underlying mental health difficulties including depression, anxiety and eating disorders. These difficulties can be seen across the whole ability range and have a continuum of severity. Attachment disorders and attention deficit disorder will also be part of this continuum. Pupils with special educational needs in this area are those who have persistent difficulties despite the school having in place an effective school behaviour policy and a robust personal and social curriculum.

### *Main characteristics*

- inattentive, poor concentration and lacking interest in school and school work
- easily frustrated and anxious about changes
- difficulty working in groups
- unable to work independently, constantly seeking help or attention
- confrontational: verbally aggressive towards pupils and/or adults
- physically aggressive towards pupils and/or adults
- destroys property: their own and that of others
- appears withdrawn, distressed, unhappy, or sulky, and may self-harm
- lacks confidence and self-esteem
- may find it difficult to communicate
- finds it difficult to accept praise

### *How can the PE teacher help?*

- Check the ability level of the pupil and adapt the level of work to this.
- Consider the pupil's strengths and use them.
- Tell the pupil what you expect in advance, as regards work and behaviour.
- Talk to the pupil to find out a bit about them.
- Set a subject target with a reward system, but be aware of general behaviour targets so PE can contribute to overall development.
- Focus your comments on the behaviour not on the pupil and offer an alternative way of behaving when correcting the pupil.
- Avoid situations where the pupil stands out from their peers.
- Use positive language and verbal praise whenever possible.
- Tell the pupil what you want them to do: 'I need you to . . .', 'I want you to . . .', rather than ask. This avoids confrontation and allows the possibility that there is room for negotiation.
- Give the pupil a choice between two options.
- Stick to what you say.

- Involve the pupil in responsibilities to increase self-esteem and confidence.
- Plan a 'time out' system; ask a colleague for help with this.
- In competitive situations, focus on individual progress rather than an outcome in terms of winning, losing – scoring/conceding. Targets relating to individual controllables, such as fitness, can also be used, and 'non-team' activities, such as dance, gymnastics, swimming and athletics, are often ways of engaging children with these difficulties.

**Further information**

SEBDA 01233 622958 www.sebda.org

## Sensory impairments

### *Hearing impairment (HI)*

The term 'hearing impairment' is a generic term used to describe all hearing loss. The main types of loss are monaural, conductive, sensory and mixed loss. The degree of hearing loss is described as mild, moderate, severe or profound. Some children rely on lip reading, others will use hearing aids, and a small proportion will have British Sign Language (BSL) as their primary means of communication.

#### *How can the PE teacher help?*

- Check the degree of loss the pupil has.
- Check the best position in team games – is hearing better on the left or right?
- Check that the pupil can see your face for facial expressions and lip reading.
- Provide a list of vocabulary, context and visual clues, especially for new sports/games.
- During class discussion allow one pupil to speak at a time and indicate where the speaker is.
- Allow for the development of a number of non-verbal communication methods between pupils involved in activities.
- Check that any aids are working and if there is any other specialist equipment available.

**Further information**

| | | |
|---|---|---|
| Action on Hearing Loss | 020 7296 8000 | www.actiononhearingloss.org.uk |
| The National Deaf Children's Society | 020 7490 8656 | www.ndcs.org.uk |

### *Visual impairment (VI)*

Visual impairment refers to a range of difficulties, including those pupils with monocular vision (vision in one eye), those who are partially sighted and those who are blind. Pupils with visual impairment cover the whole ability range and some pupils may have other SEN.

### *How can the PE teacher help?*

- Check the optimum position for the pupil, e.g. for a monocular pupil their good eye should be towards the action.
- Always provide the pupil with his own copy of rules, etc.
- Provide enlarged print copies of written text.
- Check use of ICT (enlarged icons, talking text).
- Do not stand with your back to the window/sun as this creates a silhouette and makes it harder for the pupil to see you.
- Draw the pupil's attention to displays – which they may not notice.
- Make sure the floor is kept free of clutter.
- Tell the pupil if there is a change to the layout of a space.
- Ask if there is any specialist equipment available (e.g. enlarged print dictionaries, balls with bells or rice to enable movement to be tracked).
- Manual guidance can assist skill development, so you might, for instance, put your hand together with theirs to demonstrate a tennis forehand or a swimming stroke. Always ensure that another adult (teaching assistant, teacher) is present and check the school's policy on manual guidance, before using this strategy.

**Further information**

| | | |
|---|---|---|
| Royal National Institute for Blind People RNIB | 0303 123 9999 | www.rnib.org.uk |

## ***Multi-sensory impairment***

Pupils with multi-sensory impairment have a combination of visual and hearing difficulties. They may also have other additional disabilities that make their situation complex. A pupil with these difficulties is likely to have a high level of individual support.

### *How can the PE teacher help?*

- The PE teacher will need to liaise with support staff to ascertain the appropriate provision within each subject.
- Consideration will need to be given to alternative means of communication.
- Be prepared to be flexible and to adapt tasks, targets and assessment procedures.

## Specific learning difficulties (SpLD)

The term 'specific learning difficulties' covers dyslexia, dyscalculia and dyspraxia.

### *Dyslexia*

The term 'dyslexia' is used to describe difficulties that affect the ability to learn to read, write and/or spell stemming from a difficulty in processing the sounds in words. Although found across a whole range of ability, pupils with dyslexia often have strengths in reasoning and in visual and creative skills, but their particular difficulties can result in underachievement in school. While pupils can learn strategies to manage the effects of dyslexia, it is a life-long condition and its effects may be amplified at times of stress or in unfamiliar situations.

#### *Main characteristics*

- The pupil may frequently lose their place while reading, make frequent errors with high-frequency words and have difficulty reading names and blending sounds and segmenting words. Reading requires a great deal of effort and concentration.
- The pupil's written work may seem messy, with crossings out, and similarly shaped letters may be confused, such as b/d/p/q, m/w, n/u, and letters in words may be jumbled, such as tired/tried. Spelling difficulties often persist into adult life and these pupils become reluctant writers.
- Personal organisation can be underdeveloped.

#### *How can the PE teacher help?*

- Be aware of the type of difficulty and the pupil's strengths.
- Allow the use of word processing, spell checkers and computer-aided learning packages.
- Provide word lists and photocopies of rules, etc.
- Consider alternative recording methods, e.g. pictures, plans, flow charts, mind maps.
- Allow extra time for tasks, including assessments and examinations.
- Provide reminders to bring kit, dates of sports fixtures, etc.
- Be aware of potential problems if asking pupils to record results.

**Further information**

www.bdadyslexia.org.uk

## *Dyscalculia*

The term 'dyscalculia' is used to describe difficulties in processing number concepts and mastering basic numeracy skills. These difficulties might be in marked contrast to the pupil's developmental level and general ability in other areas.

### *Main characteristics*

- *In number*, the pupil may have difficulty counting by rote, writing or reading numbers, miss out or reverse numbers, have difficulty with mental maths, and be unable to remember concepts, rules and formulae.
- *In maths-based concepts*, the pupil may have difficulty with money, telling the time, with directions, right and left, and with sequencing events, or may lose track of turns, e.g. in team games, dance.
- Poor time management and organisational skills.

### *How can the PE teacher help?*

- Provide photocopies of number/word lists and rules.
- Make use of ICT and teach the use of calculators.
- Plan the setting out of work, with it well spaced on the page.
- Allow extra time for tasks, including assessments and examinations.
- Asking children to keep score during a game could prove difficult – consider tallying systems, automatic counters, etc.

**Further information**

www.dyscalculia.co.uk

## *Dyspraxia*

The term 'dyspraxia' is used to describe an immaturity in the way in which the brain processes information, resulting in messages not being properly transmitted.

### *Main characteristics*

- difficulty in co-ordinating movements, may appear awkward and clumsy
- difficulty with handwriting and drawing, throwing and catching
- difficulty following sequential events, e.g. multiple instructions
- may misinterpret situations, take things literally
- limited social skills, resulting in frustration and irritability
- some articulation difficulties

### *How can the PE teacher help?*

- Be sensitive to the pupil's limitations in games and outdoor activities and plan tasks to enable success.
- Ask the pupil questions to check his understanding of instructions/tasks.
- Check seating position to encourage good presentation (both feet resting on the floor, desk at elbow height and ideally with a sloping surface to work on).
- Allow basic facets of skills to be utilised – so sending, receiving from a still or seated position – through to bounce passes and target games, rather than throwing/catching games.

**Further information**

Dyspraxia Foundation 01462 455 016 www.dyspraxiafoundation.org.uk

## Speech, language and communication difficulties (SLCD)

Pupils with speech, language and communication difficulties have problems that affect the full range of communication and the development of skills may be significantly delayed. Such difficulties are very common in young children but most problems are resolved during the primary years. Problems that persist beyond the transfer to secondary school will be more severe and will have a significant effect on self-esteem and personal and social relationships. The development of literacy skills is also likely to be affected. Even where pupils learn to decode, they may not understand what they have read. Sign language and symbols offer pupils an additional method of communication.

Pupils with speech, language and communication difficulties cover the whole range of academic abilities.

### *Main characteristics*

- Speech difficulties: difficulties with expressive language may involve problems in articulation and the production of speech sounds, or in co-ordinating the muscles that control speech. Pupils may have a stammer or some other form of dysfluency.
- Language/communication difficulties: receptive language impairments lead to difficulty in understanding other people. Pupils may use words incorrectly with inappropriate grammatical patterns, have a reduced vocabulary, or find it hard to recall words and express ideas. Some pupils will also have difficulty using and understanding eye contact, facial expression, gesture and body language.

### *How can the PE teacher help?*

- Talk to parents, speech therapist – and the pupil.
- Learn the most common signs for your subject.
- Use visual supports: objects, pictures, symbols.
- Use the pupil's name when addressing them.
- Give one instruction at a time, using short, simple sentences.
- Make sure the pupil has understood what they have to do before beginning.
- Provide a good model of spoken language and rephrase the pupil's response where appropriate: 'I think you are saying . . .'
- Give time for the pupil to respond before repeating a question.
- Make sure pupils understand what they have to do before starting a task.
- Pair with a work/subject buddy.
- Give access to a computer or other IT equipment appropriate to the subject.
- Give written homework instructions.

**Further information**

| | | |
|---|---|---|
| I CAN | 0845 225 4073 or 020 7843 2552 | www.ican.org.uk |
| AFASIC | 0300 666 9410 (Helpline) | www.afasic.org.uk |

## Tourette's syndrome (TS)

Tourette's syndrome (TS) is a neurological disorder characterised by tics – involuntary rapid or sudden movements or sounds that are frequently repeated. There is a wide range of severity of the condition, with some people having no need to seek medical help while others have a socially disabling condition. The tics can be suppressed for a short time but will be more noticeable when the pupil is anxious or excited.

### *Main characteristics*

- *Physical tics* range from simple blinking or nodding through more complex movements to more extreme conditions such as echopraxia (imitating actions seen) or copropraxia (repeatedly making obscene gestures).
- *Vocal tics* may be as simple as throat clearing or coughing but can progress to be as extreme as echolalia (the repetition of what was last heard) or coprolalia (the repetition of obscene words).

TS itself causes no behavioural or educational problems but other associated disorders, such as attention deficit hyperactivity disorder (ADHD) or obsessive compulsive disorder (OCD), may be present.

### *How can the PE teacher help?*

- Establish a rapport with the pupil.
- Talk to the parents.
- Agree an 'escape route' signal, should the tics become disruptive.
- Allow the pupil to sit at the back of the room to prevent staring, and avoid asking him to 'demonstrate' positions etc. unless he volunteers.
- Give access to a computer to reduce handwriting.
- Make sure the pupil is not teased or bullied or put in a situation where they may feel vulnerable.
- Be alert for signs of anxiety or depression.

**Further information**

| | | |
|---|---|---|
| Tourettes Action | UK 0300 777 8427 (Helpdesk) | www.tourettes-action.org.uk |

# Appendix 4 Strategic planner for inclusion

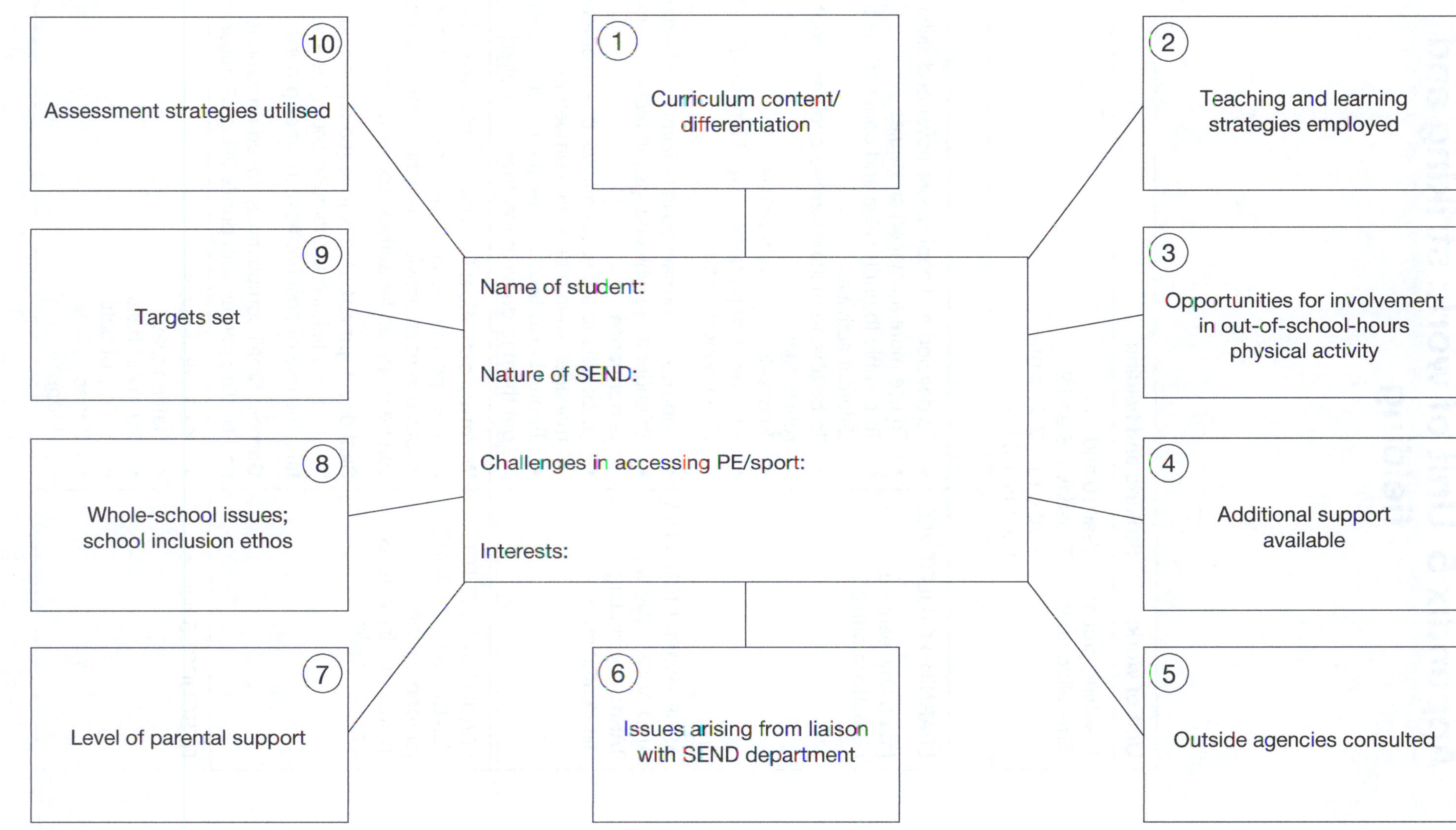

# Appendix 5 Unit of work: striking and fielding

| **Unit of work:** | **Striking and fielding** |
|---|---|
| Teaching group:<br>Time allocated: | Year 10 and 11<br>Tuesday P 8 and 9<br>2.30 p.m. – 3.30 p.m.<br>6 x 1 hr = 6 hrs |

| | |
|---|---|
| LEARNING OBJECTIVES<br><br>(mark key learning objectives with a*) | • To develop and apply more advanced skills<br>• To use more advanced strategies<br>• To be able to apply rules and conventions to different activities<br>• To be able to make informed choices about what role to take<br>• To develop leadership skills<br>• To know how preparation and fitness relate to and affect performance |
| ASSESSMENT CRITERIA AND ASSESSMENT TASKS – including differentiation | • Improve performances in striking and fielding<br>• To understand why changes in technique improve performance<br>• To be able to act as an official, coach or team manager when others are competing<br>• To be able to take charge of a group of peers and get them to do whatever task is required |
| LEARNING ACTIVITIES/ TEACHING METHODS (chronologically) – including differentiated learning tasks | **Warm-up activities:** Fielding-based pulse raiser. Activity specific stretching. Identify key muscles involved in each activity. How these muscle groups can be prepared for activity and developed.<br><br>**Skill development:** Pupils to research batting, bowling and fielding techniques and rules and then to take the role of coach/official in small groups.<br><br>**Games:** Small competitions based on various striking and fielding games with pupils filling all major roles. |
| RESOURCES needed | • Kwik cricket sets<br>• Batting tees<br>• Variety of balls<br>• Variety of bats<br>• Cones<br>• Hoops |

<table>
<tr><td>ROLE OF SUPPORT STAFF</td><td>

- Assist various pupils
- Assist in putting equipment out and away
- Enable pupils to communicate
- Ensure safe practice

</td></tr>
<tr><td>CROSS-CURRICULAR (PSE, IT)</td><td>

**English:** Speaking and listening.

**Mathematics:** Scoring.

**Science:** How the body works, warm-up.

**PSHE:** Self-esteem, positive self-concept.

**RE:** Spiritual: enjoyment of learning. Moral: consideration of others. Honesty, integrity, turn-taking, co-operation.

**Equal opportunities:** Access for all (see access strategies). Opportunity to play and act as an official.

**ICT:** Data recording and activity research via the Internet.

</td></tr>
<tr><td colspan="2">

**ACCESS STRATEGIES**: To establish the optimum roles in striking and fielding games for all pupils and to encourage them to learn the key requirements of each task. Utilise techniques from JSLA to encourage pupils to become good sports leaders. Set up Top Link management teams to utilise the new skills developed and organise sports events.

</td></tr>
</table>

# Appendix 6 Unit of work: football

| **Unit of work:** | **Games: football** |
|---|---|
| Teaching group:<br>Time allocated: | Year 7, 8 and 9<br>Friday<br>9.30 – 10.30 a.m.<br>4 x 1 hr = 4 hrs |

| | |
|---|---|
| LEARNING OBJECTIVES (mark key learning objectives with a*) | • To develop skills in travelling with the ball<br>• To pass and receive a ball with a partner<br>• To control a ball moving towards them in a number of ways<br>• To shoot from a stationary/moving position<br>• To play a small-sided game and know the rules |
| ASSESSMENT CRITERIA AND ASSESSMENT TASKS – including differentiation | • Know how and why we warm up<br>• Can travel with a ball with some control<br>• Can pass and receive a ball<br>• Uses tactics to attack and defend<br>• Evaluates their play |
| LEARNING ACTIVITIES/ TEACHING METHODS (chronologically) – including differentiated learning tasks | **Warm-up games**<br>1. Co-operative games<br>2. Warm-up exercises<br>**BASIC SKILLS AND TECHNIQUES**<br>**1. Travelling with the ball**<br>• Maintaining control<br>• Varying pace and direction<br>• Beating an opponent<br>**2. Passing the ball**<br>• Different shots<br>• Angles<br>• Accuracy<br>• Getting free<br>**3. Controlling the ball**<br>• Different body parts<br>• Control/move/pass<br>**4. Heading**<br>• In attack<br>• In defence<br>• As a pass |

<table>
<tr><td></td><td>5. Shooting<ul><li>Power v. accuracy</li><li>Aiming at a target/skittle/goal</li></ul>6. Tackling<ul><li>Front/side</li><li>Intercepting</li></ul>7. Goalkeeping<ul><li>Collecting the ball at various heights/directions</li><li>Positioning</li><li>Blocking the shot</li></ul>TACTICS AND TEAM SKILLS<br>1. Principles of play<ul><li>Simple principles of attack and defence</li></ul>2. Systems of play<ul><li>Simple formations</li></ul>3. Set plays<ul><li>Throw-ins, corners, starts–re-starts</li></ul>BASIC RULES OF THE GAME (5-a-side)<ul><li>Small-sided game</li><li>Agreed adapted rules</li></ul></td></tr>
<tr><td>RESOURCES needed</td><td><ul><li>Footballs</li><li>Marker cones</li><li>Coloured bibs</li></ul></td></tr>
<tr><td>ROLE OF SUPPORT STAFF</td><td><ul><li>Staff to support students with verbal prompts for understanding of tasks</li><li>Assist [pupil's name] with equipment</li><li>Assist in game scenarios</li></ul></td></tr>
<tr><td>CROSS-CURRICULAR (PSE, IT)</td><td>English: Speaking and listening.<br>Mathematics: Scoring.<br>Science: How the body works, warm-up.<br>PSHE: Self-esteem, positive self-concept.<br>RE: Spiritual: enjoyment of learning. Moral: consideration of others. Promoting honesty and integrity. Social: turn-taking, co-operation.<br>Equal opportunities: Access for all (see access strategies). Opportunity to play and act as an official.</td></tr>
<tr><td colspan="2">ACCESS STRATEGIES: Teacher and support staff to work with all pupils, ensuring understanding of tasks and giving verbal prompts where necessary. After four weeks, a mixed-ability Year 7, 8 and 9 group will be able to play an adapted indoor game.</td></tr>
</table>

# Appendix 7 Unit of work: aiming games

| Unit of work: | **Aiming games: Skittles, New Age Kurling, Target Frisbee/ Boccia** |
|---|---|
| Teaching group:<br>Time allocated: | Year 7, 8 and 9<br>Friday P 1 and 2<br>9.30 a.m. – 10.30 a.m.<br>6 x 1 hr = 6 hrs |

| | |
|---|---|
| LEARNING OBJECTIVES<br>(mark key learning objectives with a*) | • To improve their skills in three aiming games<br>• To use tactics and strategies to win the game<br>• To make decisions about their role in each activity<br>• To take a leading role, judge a performance and decide how to improve it<br>• To be able to select activities which prepare them for aiming games |
| ASSESSMENT CRITERIA AND ASSESSMENT TASKS – including differentiation | • Take part in/lead warm-up sessions<br>• Demonstrate good technique by improving their scores in all/two/one activity/ies<br>• Plan and implement a game plan<br>• Act as an official/coach and provide feedback |
| LEARNING ACTIVITIES/ TEACHING METHODS (chronologically) – including differentiated learning tasks | **Warm-up activities:** Aerobic warm-up to music: pulse raise, lift, circle, shake and stretch. Taking the lead for parts of the warm-up. Leading stretches, considering suitable warm-up for the activity.<br>**Development:** Skill practices for each activity. Roles: competitor, coach, recorder/scorer.<br>**Games:** All three activities parallel, rotate after competition.<br>**Concluding activities:** Calm music, stretches. |
| RESOURCES needed | • CD and player (Cae)<br>• Skittles<br>• Benches<br>• Playground chalk<br>• New Age Kurling stones, senders and target<br>• Frisbees (foam and plastic)<br>• Laminated numbers |
| ROLE OF SUPPORT STAFF | All to assist in retrieving equipment, provide prompts to improve play and in recording scores/results. |
| CROSS-CURRICULAR (PSE, IT) | **ICT:** Recording own personal best performances.<br>**Equal opportunities:** (See 'Access strategies' below.) Opportunity to act as an official, recorder. |
| **ACCESS STRATEGIES**: Group 1: Assistive device for Skittles and Kurling and an enabler where necessary. Group 2: Assistive device without enabler. Group 3: Chair close by to hold balls, assistance to retrieve the balls/Kurling stones. Group 4: Independent participation with some verbal prompts. | |

# Appendix 8 Unit of work: Table Cricket

| **Unit of work:** | **Games: Table Cricket** |
|---|---|
| Teaching group:<br>Time allocated: | Year 7, 8 and 9<br>Friday<br>2.00 p.m. – 3.00 p.m.<br>6 x 1 hr = 6 hrs |

| | |
|---|---|
| LEARNING OBJECTIVES<br>(mark key learning objectives with a*) | • To prepare for each activity and recover afterwards<br>• To learn the rules and scoring systems of Table Cricket<br>• To develop techniques, tactics and strategies<br>• To play and compete with positive attitudes, displaying honest competition and good sporting behaviour |
| ASSESSMENT CRITERIA AND ASSESSMENT TASKS – including differentiation | • Warms up for each lesson<br>• Knows basic rules<br>• Knows own strengths<br>• Observes and evaluates others<br>• Wins/loses graciously; shakes hands with opponents, three cheers, etc. |
| LEARNING ACTIVITIES/ TEACHING METHODS (chronologically) – including differentiated learning tasks | **Warm-up**: Upper body warm-up based on shake, circle, lift, stretch to involve all arm and hand joints, head, shoulders and trunk; sometimes to music, sometimes pupils lead.<br>**Table Cricket:**<br>• **Bowling:** learning to use fast, spin ball, set the field<br>• **Batting:** aiming to score 4s, leave wide balls, learning to avoid the active fielder<br>• **Fielding:** practise moving the fielders as directed by the captain; practise being the active fielder<br>**Game:** play 1 v. 1, ability paired, play team v. team over a number of weeks<br>• Learn to fill in the score sheet. |
| RESOURCES needed | • Coomber and modern music tapes<br>• Table tennis table<br>• Table Cricket equipment<br>• Scoring sheets (Table Cricket)<br>• Table Cricket rule book |
| ROLE OF SUPPORT STAFF | • Act as an official<br>• Assist moving fielders (TC)<br>• Assist in putting equipment out and away<br>• Enable pupils to communicate<br>• Record scores |

*(Continued)*

*(Continued)*

| CROSS-CURRICULAR (PSE, IT) | **Equal opportunities:** All pupils take part (see access strategies).<br><br>**RE:** Spiritual: enjoyment of learning. Moral: consideration towards others; promoting honesty and integrity.<br>Cultural: develop positive self-concept.<br><br>**Maths:** Scoring; angles; timing. |
|---|---|
| **ACCESS STRATEGIES**: All bags removed from the chairs. Tray removed for Table Cricket. Chest harness removed for Table Cricket to enable pupil to get closer to the table. | |

# Appendix 9 Individual checklist for inclusion in PE and sport

NAME:__________________________________ YEAR GROUP: _____________

NATURE OF SEND/PROBLEMS OF ACCESS TO PHYSICAL ACTIVITY:______

______________________________________________________________

EXISTING INTERESTS: ___________________________________________

______________________________________________________________

On a sliding scale of 1–10 (1 being poor, through below satisfactory, satisfactory – good – right through to 10 as excellent), how does the student rate for each of these indicators?

| INDICATOR OF HIGH-QUALITY PE AND SPORT | RATING |
|---|---|
| • Committed, making PE and sport a central part of life in and out of school | |
| • Knows and understands what they are trying to achieve and how to go about doing it | |
| • Understands that PE and sport are an important part of an active, healthy lifestyle | |
| • Has the confidence to get involved | |
| • Has the skills and control to take part | |
| • Willingly takes part in a range of group and individual activities | |
| • Can think about what they are doing and make appropriate decisions for themselves | |
| • Wants to improve and achieve in relation to own abilities | |
| • Has the stamina, suppleness and strength to keep going | |
| • Enjoys PE, school and community sport | |

# Useful contacts

## National governing bodies of sport

All England Netball Association – www.england-netball.co.uk
Amateur Rowing Association (ARA) – www.ara-rowing.org
Amateur Swimming Association – www.britishswimming.org
Badminton Association of England – www.badmintonengland.co.uk/homepage.asp
Baseball Softball UK and Major League Baseball – www.BaseballSoftballUK.com
British Cycling Federation – www.bcf.uk.com
British Gymnastics – www.british-gymnastics.org
British Triathlon Association – www.britishtriathlon.org
England and Wales Cricket Board (ECB) – www.ecb.co.uk
England Squash – www.squash.co.uk
English Basketball Association – www.basketballengland.org.uk
English Lacrosse Association – www.englishlacrosse.co.uk
English Table Tennis Association – www.etta.co.uk
English Volleyball Association – www.volleyballengland.org
Football Association – www.the-fa.org
Golf Foundation – www.golf-foundation.org
Hockey England – www.hockeyonline.co.uk
Lawn Tennis Association – www.lta.org.uk
National Rounders Association – www.NRA-rounders.co.uk
Rugby Football League – www.sporting-life.com/rugbyleague
Rugby Football Union – www.rfu.com
UK Athletics – www.ukathletics.net

English Federation of Disability Sport – www.efds.co.uk – This website contains numerous links to a host of organisations involved in the promotion of sporting and other opportunities for young people with disabilities.

## Professional subject organisations

The Association for Physical Education – www.afpe.org.uk/

## National sports organisations

British Olympic Association (BOA) – www.olympics.org.uk
British Paralympic Association (BPA) – www.paralympics.org.uk
British Sports Trust (BST) – www.bstorg.uk

UK Coaching – www.ukcoaching.org
Women's Sports Foundation – www.wsf.org.uk
Youth Sport Trust – www.youthsporttrust.org

# References and further reading

## Teaching and learning – general

Armour, K. (2011) *Sport Pedagogy: An Introduction for Teaching and Coaching*, Essex: Pearson.

Armour, K. (2014) *Pedagogical Cases in Physical Education and Youth Sport*, London: Routledge.

Bailey, R. and Kirk, D. (2009) *The Routledge Physical Education Reader*, London: Routledge.

Children and Families Act 2014, www.legislation.gov.uk/ukpga/2014/6/contents/enacted

DfE (2015) Special Educational Needs and Disability Code of Practice: 0 to 25 Years, London: DfE Publications, www.gov.uk/government/publications/send-code-of-practice-0-to-25

Equality Act 2010, www.gov.uk/guidance/equality-act-2010-guidance

Frapwell, A. (2014) *A Practical Guide to Assessing Without Levels*, Leeds: Coachwise.

Graham, G. M. (2008) *Teaching Children Physical Education: Becoming a Master Teacher*, Leeds: Human Kinetics.

Griffin, L. L. and Butler, J. I. (2010) *More Teaching Games for Understanding: Moving Globally*, Champaign, IL: Human Kinetics.

Grout, H. and Long, G. (2009) *Improving Teaching and Learning in Physical Education*, Maidenhead: Open University Press.

Hay, P. and Penney, D. (2012) *Assessment in Physical Education: A Socio-cultural Perspective*, London: Routledge.

Kirk, D., Macdonald, D. and O'Sullivan, M. (2006) *Handbook of Physical Education*, London: Sage.

Laker, A. (2001) *Developing Personal, Social and Moral Education through Physical Education: A Practical Guide for Teachers*, London: Routledge.

Lavin, J. (2008) *Creative Approaches to Physical Education: Helping Children to Achieve Their True Potential*, London: Routledge.

Light, R. (2013) *Game Sense: Pedagogy for Performance, Participation and Enjoyment*, London: Routledge.

Mosston, M. and Ashworth, S. (2001) *Teaching Physical Education*, San Francisco, CA: Benjamin Cummings.

Pickard, A. and Maude, P. (2014) *Teaching Physical Education Creatively*, London: Routledge.

Rink, J. (2008) *Physical Education Curriculum*, New York: McGraw-Hill.

Stidder, G. (2015) *Becoming a Physical Educator*, London: Routledge.

Stidder, G. and Binney, J. (2012) *Innovative Approaches to Teaching and Learning in Physical Education*, London: Routledge.

Stolz, S. A. (2014) *The Philosophy of Physical Education: A New Perspective*, London: Routledge.
Tinning, R. (2011) *Pedagogy and Human Movement*, London: Routledge.
Webster, M. and Misra, S. (2015) *Teaching the Primary Foundation Subjects*, Maidenhead: McGraw-Hill Education.

## Research and contemporary issues

Armour, K. and Macdonald, D. (2012) *Research Methods in Physical Education and Youth Sport*, London: Routledge.
Bailey, R. and Kirk, D. (2009) *The Routledge Physical Education Reader*, London: Routledge.
Blatchford, P., Bassett, P., Brown, P., Martin, C., Russell, A. and Webster, R. (2009) The Deployment and Impact of Support Staff Project: Research Brief (DCSF-RB148). London: Department for Children, Schools and Families.
Capel, S. and Pitrowski, S. (2013) *Issues in Physical Education*, London: Routledge.
Capel, S. and Whitehead, M. (2012) *Debates in Physical Education*, London: Routledge.
Dyson, B. and Casey, A. (2014) *Cooperative Learning in Physical Education: A Research Based Approach*, London: Routledge.
Green, K. (2008) *Understanding Physical Education*, London: Sage.
Hardman, K. and Green, K. (2011) *Contemporary Issues in Physical Education: International Perspectives*, Maidenhead: Meyer & Meyer.
Kirk, D. (2013) *Physical Education and Curriculum Study*, London: Routledge.
O'Sullivan, M. and MacPhail, A. (2010) *Young People's Voices in Physical Education and Youth Sport*, London: Routledge.
Ovens, A., Hopper, T. and Butler, J. (2012) *Complexity Thinking in Physical Education: Reframing Curriculum, Pedagogy and Research*, London: Routledge.
Piper, H. (2015) *Touch in Sports Coaching and Physical Education: Fear, Risk and Moral Panic*, London: Routledge.
Piper, H., Garratt, D. and Taylor, B. (2015) *Moral Panic in Physical Education and Coaching*, London: Routledge.
Rossi, T., Hunter, L., Christensen, E. and Macdonald, D. (2014) *Workplace Learning in Physical Education: Emerging Teachers' Stories from the Staffroom and Beyond*, London: Routledge.
Russell, A. Webster, R. and Blatchford, P. (2013) *Maximising the Impact of Teaching Assistants*, London: Routledge.
Tannehill, D., MacPhail, A., Halbert G. and Murphy, F. (2012) *Research and Practice in Physical Education*, London: Routledge.
Whitehead, J., Telfer, H. and Lambert, J. (2013) *Values in Youth Sport and Physical Education*, London: Routledge.
Wright, J., Macdonald, D. and Burrows, L. (2004) *Critical Inquiry and Problem-Solving in Physical Education*, London: Routledge.

## Movement and motor development

Colvin, V. A., Markos, N. and Walker, P. (2008) *Teaching the Nuts and Bolts of Physical Education: Ages 5–12* (2nd edn), Champaign, IL: Human Kinetics.
Gallahue D. L. (2002) *Developmental Physical Education for Today's Children*, Champaign, IL: Human Kinetics.
Gallahue, D. L. and Cleland-Donnelly, F. (2007) *Developmental Physical Education for All Children*, Champaign, IL: Human Kinetics.
Gallahue, D. L. and Ozmun, J. C. (2011) *Understanding Motor Development: Infants, Children. Adolescents, Adults* (7th edn), London: McGraw-Hill.

Graham, G., Holt/Hale, S. A. and Parker, M. (2012) *Children Moving: A Reflective Approach to Teaching Physical Education* (9th edn), New York: McGraw-Hill.
Haywood, K. and Getchell, N. (2009) *Life Span Motor Development* (5th edn), Leeds: Human Kinetics.
Whitehead, M. (2010) *Physical Literacy Throughout the Lifecourse*, London: Routledge.

## Inclusive practice

Addy, L. M. (2006) *Get Physical! An Inclusive, Therapeutic P.E. Programme to Develop Motor Skills*, Cambridge: LDA.
Grenier, M. (2014) *Physical Education for Students with Autism Spectrum Disorders*, Leeds: Human Kinetics.
Horvat, M., Kalakian, L., Croce, R. and Dahlstrom, V. (2010) *Developmental/Adapted Physical Education Making Ability Count* (5th edn), San Francisco, CA: Benjamin Cummings.
Morley, D. and Bailey, R. (2006) *Meeting the Needs of Your Most Able Pupils: Physical Education and Sport*, London: David Fulton.
Rouse, P. (2009) *Inclusion in Physical Education*, Leeds: Human Kinetics.
Stidder, G. and Hayes, S. (2012) *Equity and Inclusion in Physical Education and Sport*, London: Routledge.
Vickerman, P. (2006) *Teaching Physical Education to Children with Special Educational Needs*, London: Routledge.

## Subject leadership

Frapwell, A. and Caldecott, S. (2011) *In Deep: Learning to Learn in Physical Education*, Leeds: Coachwise.
Haydn-Davies, D. and Kaitell, E. (2010) *Physical Education: Beyond the Curriculum*, Leeds: Coachwise.
Lund, J. and Tannehill, D. (2014) *Standards-Based Physical Education Curriculum Development*, Boston, MA: Jones and Bartlett Publishers.
Severs, J. (2012) *Safety and Risk in Primary School Physical Education*, London: Routledge.
Whitlam, P. (2012) *Safe Practice in Physical Education and Sport*, Leeds: Coachwise.
Wilkinson, S., Marchant, E. and Hunt, M. (2009) *A Practical Guide to Achieving Excellence and High Quality Leadership in Primary Physical Education*, Leeds: Coachwise.

## Early years and physical development

Cooper, L. and Doherty, J. (2010) *Physical Development: Supporting Development in the Early Years Foundation Stage*, London: Continuum.
Davies, M. (2003) *Movement and Dance in Early Childhood* (2nd edn), London: Sage Publications.
Doherty, J. and Bailey, R. (2002) *Supporting Physical Development in the Early Years*, Buckingham: Open University Press.
Pica, R. (2014) *Early Elementary Children Moving and Learning: A Physical Education Curriculum*, Saint Paul, MN: Redleaf Press.
Wetton, P. (1997) *Physical Education in the Early Years*, London: Routledge.

## Physical education – health related texts

Association for Physical Education (October 2015) Health Position Paper, www.afpe.org.uk/physical-education/wp-content/uploads/afPE_Health_Position_Paper_Web_Version2015.pdf (accessed 3 May 2017).

BHFNC (March 2013) Interpreting the UK physical activity guidelines for children, www.ssehsactive.org.uk/young-people-latest-news-item/368/index.html

Booth, J.N., Leary, S.D., Joinson, C., *et al.* (2003) Associations between Objectively Measured Physical Activity and Academic Attainment in Adolescents from a UK Cohort. *British Journal of Sports Medicine*. Published Online First: 22 October 2013. doi: 10.1136/bjsports-2013-092334

Cale, L. and Harris, J. (2005) *Exercise and Young People: Issues, Implications and Initiatives*, Basingstoke: Palgrave Macmillan.

Department of Health (2011) Start Active, Stay Active: A Report on Physical Activity for Health from the Four Home Countries Chief Medical Officers, www.gov.uk/government/publications/start-active-stay-active-a-report-on-physical-activity-from-the-four-home-countries-chief-medical-officers (accessed 3 May 2017).

Dinan Thompson, M. (Ed.) (2009) *Physical Education and Health: Issues for Curriculum in Australia and New Zealand*, Melbourne, Victoria: Oxford University Press.

Elbourn, J. (2008) *Aerobics and Circuits for Secondary Schools*, Leeds: Coachwise.

Elbourn, J. and James, A. (2013) *Fitness Room Activities for Secondary Schools: A Guide to Promoting Learning about Healthy Active Lifestyles*, Leeds: Coachwise.

Public Health England (2014) The Link between Pupil Health and Wellbeing and Attainment – a Briefing for Head Teachers, Governors and Staff in Education Settings, www.gov.uk/government/publications/the-link-between-pupil-health-and-wellbeing-and-attainment (accessed 8 May 2017).

## Primary physical education – initial teacher education

Allen, W. (2009) *Classroom Gems: Games, Ideas and Activities for Primary PE*, Essex: Pearson.

Armour, K. (2012) *Sport Pedagogy: An Introduction for Teaching and Coaching,* Essex: Pearson.

Bailey, R. (2001) *Teaching Physical Education: A Handbook for Primary and Secondary School Teachers*, London: Kogan.

Doherty, J. and Brennan, P. (2013) *Physical Education 5–11: A Guide for Teachers*, London: Routledge.

Gallahue, D. L. and Ozmun, J. C. (2011) *Understanding Motor Development: Infants, Children, Adolescents, Adults* (7th edn), London: McGraw-Hill.

Graber, K. and Woods, A. (2012) *Physical Education and Activity for Elementary Classroom Teachers*, New York: McGraw-Hill.

Graham, G., Holt/Hale, S. A. and Parker, M. (2012) *Children Moving: A Reflective Approach to Teaching Physical Education* (9th edn), New York: McGraw-Hill.

Griggs, G. (2012) *An Introduction to Primary Physical Education*, London: Routledge.

Griggs, G. (2015) *Understanding Primary Physical Education*, London: Routledge.

Haywood, K. and Getchell, N. (2009) *Life Span Motor Development* (5th edn), Leeds: Human Kinetics.

Knight, E. and Chedzoy, S. (2013) *Physical Education in Primary School: Access for All*, London: David Fulton Publishers.

Lawrence, J. (2012) *Teaching Primary Physical Education*, London: Sage.

Paine, L. (2014) *Complete Guide to Primary Dance*, Leeds: Human Kinetics and NDTA.

Pangrazi, R. and Beighle, A. (2013) *Dynamic Physical Education for Elementary School Children: Lesson Plans for Implementation*, San Francisco, CA: Benjamin Cummings.

Pica, R. (2008) *Physical Education for Young Children*, Leeds: Human Kinetics.

Pickard, A. and Maude, P. (2014) *Teaching Physical Education Creatively*, London: Routledge.

Pickup, I. and Price, L. (2007) *Teaching Physical Education in the Primary School: A Developmental Approach*, London: Continuum.

Rovegno, I. and Bandhauer, D. (2013) *Elementary Physical Education: Curriculum and Instruction*, Boston, MA: Jones and Bartlett Learning.

Severs, J. (2012) *Safety and Risk in Primary School Physical Education*, London: Routledge.

Stidder, G. and Hayes, S. (2012) *The Really Useful PE Book: Learning and Teaching 7–14 Age Range*, London: Routledge.

Williams, A. and Cliffe, J. (2011) *Primary PE: Unlocking the Potential*, Maidenhead: McGraw-Hill.

Zachopolou, E., Liukkonen, J., Pickup, I. and Tsangaridou, N. (2012) *Early Steps Physical Education Curriculum*, Leeds: Human Kinetics.

## Secondary physical education – initial teacher education

Armour, K. (2012) *Sport Pedagogy: An Introduction for Teaching and Coaching*, Essex: Pearson.

Bailey, R. (2010) *Physical Education: A Guide for Secondary Schools*, London: Continuum.

Bailey, R. and Kirk, D. (2009) *The Routledge Physical Education Reader*, London: Routledge.

Capel, S. and Breckon, P. (2013) *A Practical Guide to Teaching Physical Education in the Secondary School* (2nd edn), London: Routledge.

Capel, S. and Whitehead, M. (2013) *Learning to Teach Physical Education in the Secondary School: A Companion to School Experience* (2nd edn), London: Routledge.

Capel, S. and Whitehead, M. (2015) *Learning to Teach Physical Education in the Secondary School: A Companion to School Experience* (4th edn), London: Routledge.

Darst, P., Pangrazi, R., Sariscsany, M. J. and Brusseau, T. (2013) *Dynamic Physical Education for Secondary School Students* (7th edn), San Francisco, CA: Benjamin Cummings.

Grout, H. and Long, G. (2009) *Improving Teaching and Learning in Physical Education*, Maidenhead: Open University Press.

Macfayden, T. and Bailey, R. (2002) *Teaching Physical Education 11–18: Perspectives and Challenges*, London: Continuum.

Scheff, H., Sprague, M. and McGreevy-Nichols, S. (2014) *Experiencing Dance* (2nd edn), Champaign, IL: Human Kinetics.

Stidder, G. and Hayes, S. (2012) *Equity and Inclusion in Physical Education and Sport*, London: Routledge.

Stidder, G. and Hayes, S. (2012) *The Really Useful PE Book: Learning and Teaching 7–14 Age Range*, London: Routledge.

Vickerman, P. ( 2007) *Teaching Physical Education to Children with Special Educational Needs*, London: Routledge.

# Index